5/18/15

Hilario,
you have
been a
friend for
many years.

DO YOU SEE WHAT I SEE?

Thank you
for your
loved
li C t h l

Jim Cordero Jr.

Do You See What I See?
Copyright © 2012 by Jim Cordero Jr.

ISBN: 978-1-4675-4176-3

Publishing Consulting by Coach Writer (www.coachwriter.com)
Pentopublishing.com
Coaching by Kevis Sullivan
Cover Design by Kevis Sullivan

Printed in the United States of America
August 2012

Dedication

Love is a force that cannot be reckoned with. When it is employed in full force it can move the universe, it can alter the cosmos, and it can change destinies. It is this force that altered my existence and forever changed my course. It started with God and His love for me but it didn't stop there. God looked down from the Heavens and smiled. And before the existence of time He created. And at the perfect moment, He delivered. He delivered into my life the one woman who would stand by my side. When life seemed hopeless, she hoped. And when life told her to run, she stayed. She has seen my worst and she has brought out my best. She has been not only my soul mate but the best mother to my children a father could ask for. Thus she has given me my greatest blessings, Jessica, Yvette, Ariel and Isaac. With them and God, my life is complete. So it is to her that this labor of love is dedicated. For it is she that God used to change my life. And without her, I would not be the man I am today. So to you, Irma Cordero, I dedicate not only this book but my life.

Always and Forever.......

Acknowledgment

Dad,
You never gave up on me, though I made it hard.
Thank you!
Thank you for believing in me and thank you for being
there. I owe so much to you.
Forever grateful....
And Marge, you completed us...

Mom,
We had some tough times but in the end you always
loved me.
I'm not sure how this works but I'm hoping God will
allow you to glimpse at this page.
I wish you could've seen me now....
Love you!

Sis,
You are an inspiration.
I've seen you struggle and I've seen you triumph.
God blessed me when He joined us together.
You've shown me to never give up, no matter how hard
life gets....

Table of Contents

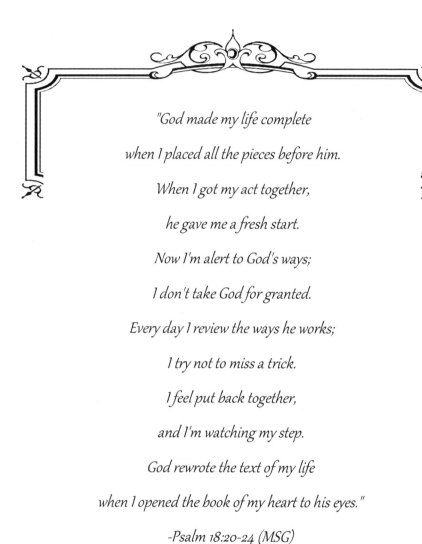

"God made my life complete

when I placed all the pieces before him.

When I got my act together,

he gave me a fresh start.

Now I'm alert to God's ways;

I don't take God for granted.

Every day I review the ways he works;

I try not to miss a trick.

I feel put back together,

and I'm watching my step.

God rewrote the text of my life

when I opened the book of my heart to his eyes."

-Psalm 18:20-24 (MSG)

Introduction

Do you see what I see? Don't we all see the same things? It's funny but I know we don't. Why? Because I don't see things in the same way as I did 30 years ago, 20 years ago, 10 years ago, or sometimes even yesterday. Seeing is about so much more than looking with the eyes. It's about opening the heart to the world around us and the one who created it. It's about facing the day and seeing the hope in the bad times and the joy in the good times. It's those little moments that make up our story and the big moments that change us forever. Why did I write this book? One day I realized I saw things differently and I knew that I needed to share this vision. It was this thought that sparked these words. My hope in this is that someone's life would be blessed by these writings and that God would give you a perfect word at the perfect moment. Jesus has done so much for me that I simply want to pay it forward as long as He allows. I pray this book will allow you to see the world as I see it, through the loving eyes of an amazing Father and Son....

Do You See What I See?

⁂ *Casting Shadows* ⁂

"So we are Christ's ambassadors; God is making his appeal through us."

-2 Corinthians 5:20 (NLT)

The thought came to me, how many people will I come in contact with today? I actually started analyzing my day to see if I could figure it out. It started with my wife of course as this is the first person I see as I wake up. Then it went to my children as they are a part of my home. Then there are my co-workers, students, peers, business contacts, all those that are associated with my place of employment. I thought if I stopped by a store, filled up my car with gas, bought lunch, this would add to the list. My mind started expanding, what about the ones that I text or email? There's still contact. Add Face book or Twitter and the number becomes exponential. Then there are the people on the road. Some might not consider them but if you've ever had someone cut you off, or better yet stop and let you into traffic, you've made contact. What about the passer-bys who I could either frown at or give a smile? I suddenly realized, I will come into contact with a multitude of people and the question came, will it be a positive interaction?

Now I started asking myself, why did this thought come? I see the concept and know that the opportunities for interaction are endless but what is the point? Then my wife walked in and I got it. I looked at her, smiled, and told her she was beautiful. Today I will rise out of bed and greet my children with a kiss and an encouraging word. When I stop at the gas station I will thank the attendant and wish them a good day. At work I will focus on the positive. And in every interaction I will ask God to help me to remember how blessed I am because I have this day in hopes that others may be blessed by our points of contact. I get it. I have a multitude of opportunities and two choices in each one, positive or negative.

Thank you for the thought Lord, I have chosen.
May they see You in me.
If they forget me, it's alright,
But may they never forget You.

May you have a wonderful day, may you see my smile through these words and may you be encouraged by these thoughts. I am blessed.
Why?
Because I know Him.
May you be blessed too!

⚜⟶ *It Happens In a Blink* ⚜⟶

"So teach us to number our days,

That we may gain a heart of wisdom."

-Psalms 90:12 (NIV)

Recently my wife came of age and entered the world of
"smart" phones. As she was playing with all the
features there were two things that enticed here and
caused this device to earn its name of being much more
than just a phone. First she realized she could listen to
her favorite contemporary Christian radio station, K-
Love, anywhere she wanted. Second she realized she
could use this feature to set up the station as an alarm
so that she could wake up to these songs every day and
I've got to admit that it is a great feature. For me these
songs have become mornings of messages from God
Himself and this morning was no different. It started
with "Blink."

"Teach me to number my days
And count every moment
Before it slips away
Take in all the colors
Before they fade to grey

I don't want to miss
Even just a second
More of this....

It happens in a blink it happens in a flash
It happens in the time it took to look back
I try to hold on tight but there's no stopping time
What is it I've done with my life?"

It caused me to go back to my childhood and recall the wonderful memories of a boy growing up and a mom who held him when he cried; a time when a trip to the zoo with my father was priceless and riding bikes with my sis was the greatest of things. Very quickly I moved forward to teenage years and the friends, cars, and rash decisions of youth. While I know now how destructive some of this time was, it was still rich with friendships gained and experiences never to be forgotten. Suddenly I was a young man and there was this girl who moved across the street...... (She's the same one who set the alarm this morning). Then the kids came, one, two, three, four; each moment so precious and each memory cherished. My mind shifted and I was taken to the moment I met Christ. As the saying goes "it was the best of times and the worst of times." My destiny changed forever as life took on new meaning. Then the lyric hit home,

"It happens in a blink it happens in a flash
It happens in the time it took to look back
I try to hold on tight but there's no stopping time
What is it I've done with my life?"

How did I get from there to here so quickly? Just yesterday I was asking my wife out for our first date and suddenly we've been married 25 years! How is it that my oldest child is 25 and my youngest about to be 16? I've experienced so much in such a short time (it seems); graduations, weddings..... And then the hard times; those have a place in this memory we call life. Now I'm starting to get a bit of anxiety. I'm nearing 50!!! It can't be!!! But it is. Finally the last line in the verse above hits, "What is it I've done with my life?" Then I add my own line, "What am I going to do with the remainder of my life?"

As anxiety mounts I am saved by God's voice speaking again through this song:

"When it's all said and done

13

No one remembers
How far we have run
The only thing that matters
Is how we have loved."

That's it!!! What am I going to do with the rest of my life? I'm going to love. I'm going to love my beautiful wife and our amazing children even more if that's at all possible. I'm going to love my friends and family. I'm going to love each and every day, no matter what it brings. Whether it's a 12 hour day at work or a day on the beach, it is the day I've been given and I'm realizing how much of a blessing each one is. And, most importantly, I'm going to love God who made all of this possible. How simple. I'm going to love.....

And all these thoughts happened "in a blink, in a flash...."
I may not be able to stop time but I can slow down enough to make sure I do the most important thing that will lead to the greatest legacy possible. I can slow down enough to love greatly each and every day.

"Slow down,
Slow down,
Before today becomes our yesterday..."

Today, slow down, love, and be blessed!
After all, we've got so much more to experience.....

(Blink by Revive)

Time To Get Busy

"What good is it, dear brothers and sisters, if you say you have faith but

don't show it by your actions? Can that kind of faith save anyone?"

-James 2:14 (NLT)

I love river walks. There is something amazing about being out in creation and sensing how we are just one part in this world that is humbling. There is also something to be said about the simplicity yet complexity of this world we live in and how we can take lessons from the creatures we share this earth with.

One day as I was enjoying one of these walks something high in the sky caught my eye. For some reason I looked up and there was a hawk simply soaring in the heavens. I began to think to myself how wonderful it must be to have the ability to rise above all things and obtain such a vision. I thought how great to be able to have a vision that could see all things for miles. I imagined how much easier it would be to reach any destination since nothing stood in the way and everything was a straight shot in any direction, no obstacles or distractions, no winding roads, simply the vision, the goal, and a direct route in between.....

But suddenly this hawk diverted. Just as majestically as it soared in the sky, it purposefully dove to the ground and before I knew it he was at my level winding between recently pruned grape vines. As he made his way through these obstacles, I realized he didn't allow these things to cause him to deviate but still flew with majesty. After a few moments of weaving in and out, he saw what he came for, pounced, and flew back to the heavens. In an instant I realized what a wonderful vision I had just been blessed with. While there was great advantage in soaring above all things, no vision or purpose could ever be obtained without getting down to earth and getting to work. In this magnificent creature I saw myself and my purpose.

I am one who needs to have a good vision of the whole picture to be productive. I am also one who appreciates having the ability to look past what is right before me to what lies ahead. With this mindset, it allows me to plan and even dream of things to come. Sometimes I can see them so clearly but I must be honest, implementing these plans and dreams is another story. Implementation always requires coming back down to the daily tasks that make up our lives and diving into the field of life with a purpose. It always has obstacles which require maneuvering around and never is a straight shot. But when the purpose is not lost, it also produces the reward of accomplishment. Then it is time to soar back up for another look around to take in the terrain, get the vision, and get back to work again. This is not a one time process but a lifetime purpose. In order to achieve my dreams and plans, I have to first see them, and then I have to get to work.

Thank you Lord for the vision, now give me the strength and tenacity to labor.

Today do not settle with always living in the tasks of the day. Allow yourself to soar to new heights and get a glimpse of what God has for you. Once you do, get to work. Life is an adventure, live it to its fullest.

Today, be blessed.

❀〜ꣴ **Slow Down** ❀〜ꣴ

"Peace, be still...."

-Mark 4:39 (KJV)

It was one of those mornings. The late night before led to the late wake-up on this day. Suddenly the eyes opened and the clock glared a time it wasn't supposed to, a time way too late and it started: the rush. For me, it's something I truly battle. I hate being late! I hate it so much it can become an obsession. It's like a spirit that comes over me and changes my complete demeanor. My heart starts pumping and my brain starts racing over all the things I have to do. In an instant my day rushes into my mind and these lost minutes somehow equate into a lost day. It's a terrible feeling....and it affects everyone around me. And it's funny because it only escalates once it starts.

I jumped up going from sound asleep to instant rush (that must do something terrible to my body). And of course everything begins to go wrong. I look for my clothes and nothing is where it's supposed to be (or I'm so hurried I look right past it). I finally make it to the shower and the water won't warm up (or I'm simply not waiting for it). I step out and cut myself shaving and it won't stop bleeding (I'm sure because my heart is racing so fast). Taking the time to make coffee or eat is out of the question so I decide to drive through Starbucks (which has a line longer than any coffee pot would have taken). They give me my order and it's wrong (so I have to park the car and go in because I'm so frustrated by now there's no way I'm leaving without my order). I go into the café and make sure they know they've made me even later (which of course really helps my testimony). Finally I'm hitting the freeway taking a large drink of my needed caffeine (as if that's what I really need....). Then the traffic, all lanes with cars doing 60 miles an hour as if there was nowhere they needed to be (their purpose must have been just to slow me down). And finally I hit my peak, I'm done, ruined, at my wits end, I'll never recover, there's too much to do in the day and I'll never meet its demands.....and finally, the voice in my head whispers,

"Peace, be still......."

Is this an exaggeration or can any of you relate? Are any of you familiar with this beast whose sole purpose is to drive you to an early grave? Its name is "Stress" and the behavior and mindset it causes can't be good. Maybe it doesn't hit you in the arena of being late to wherever, maybe it hits you at work where the duties assigned never equal the time allotted and you know you're doomed to failure. Maybe it's at home where the demands of a family all lie on your shoulders. Maybe it's the worry of what the future holds that causes your mind to race. Wherever it is it hits, it hits hard and it is destructive. If you can relate then let me share with you the One who calmed the storm and told the sea,

"Peace, be still" and it was.

On this morning it was amazing. In an instant I saw my mindset for what it was and in that same instant I felt a soothing sense of calm begin to flow through me. It started in my fingertips which loosened their grip on the steering wheel and made its way through my body. The tension started to leave and the peace began to come in. In that moment I realized that all this stress had not done anything for me. The rushing only made me later and the frustration only worsened the situation. Then it became almost comical. In fact looking back it was really funny how silly it all was, silly because all of it got me nowhere.

So today when the beast called Stress tries to sneak into your life, remember the Savior called Jesus is also standing at the door. Remember that in an instant the power that calmed the sea is available to calm your soul. Remember that whatever your circumstance is, it can be conquered. You are not alone and you are not doomed. You are blessed and you are more than a conqueror! You are a child of God and God is in control.

Remember, take a deep breath and *BE BLESSED* with His Peace!!!

❧ **The Gift** ❧

I will never forget the night. Times had been very hard. I had been in and out of the hospital for months. In fact, the last time I left the hospital, the doctor had been pretty clear. Another attack like the last one and it may be my last visit. He was so clear that he advised me to put my affairs in order. With all that in the back of my mind, I had purposed on this night to enjoy my family. It started at church. On this night I asked the Pastor if I could speak. As I made my way to the platform, it took all I had to get up the stairs. As I spoke, my breath was short. I thanked everyone for their prayers and told them I was tired. I told them I felt like that boxer on the ropes getting pummeled and I knew that God was the only thing holding me up. I hadn't given up but I had made peace. From there it was on to my daughter's softball game. I hadn't gone much lately but I wanted to see my baby play. As I sat there I was nearly overwhelmed by the thought that this could be the last game I got to watch. And there's one more important detail I can't forget. It was my wife's birthday. As I looked at her I shed a tear. Here was my struggle. I had made peace with God but I didn't want to leave my family. However, I knew the decision wasn't in my hands and I pressed forward. I remember forcing the smiles. To finish this night, we went off to a local pizzeria. It was our favorite. We went off to celebrate. And celebrate is what I decided to do. Celebrate because I knew I was a blessed man. As we got there I told my wife I wanted my pizza. She looked at me funny because she knew I was very, very limited by the doctors on what I could eat. She also looked at me funny because she knew what pizza I was talking about. When she was pregnant with our first child it was me that developed the cravings. And I craved my salami, pineapple, onion, chili and extra cheese pizza. This time she gave in. I hadn't eaten anything like that in over a year and it tasted so good. We were all together and I was glad but sad at the same time. Then it happened. The Call.

It must have been ten at night when my phone rang. My daughter answered and immediately she handed it to me. I looked down and I recognized the 415 area code as being San Francisco. I knew this was the area code of UCSF, the transplant clinic, but I couldn't bring myself to even consider it. Cautiously I remember answering. The rest is a blur. It was a doctor from the clinic and he was asking me how I was doing. He said his name was Dr. Freeze and all I could think of was the Batman movie and how this was somehow a cruel joke. I don't remember much but these words I will never forget, "We believe we have a donor and we need you at the clinic." My mind started to spin. The tears started to pour like they are as I write this. I had waited so long for this call. I had looked at my phone a million times and been disappointed a million and one. But this time, this time, God had looked down and smiled upon me and my family. I turned to my wife and somehow she

22

knew. We didn't know how to act or what emotions to feel. But we knew that the next day would change our lives forever.

Suddenly my mind shifted. A stark reality hit me. I turned to my wife and I told her, someone's dying. We all got quiet. All I could think of was that at this very moment while we were celebrating, another family was somewhere saying goodbye to their loved one. I knew this because the doctor had said they would be "harvesting the organ" in the morning. My joy was replaced by sorrow. I gathered my family and we prayed. We prayed for this individual's soul and we prayed for this family. We gave thanks for this ultimate sacrifice and wept for this ultimate loss. We had mixed feelings but we knew that because of this person's death, I was going to be given the chance to live. Even though we didn't know this individual, we knew that we would be forever connected.

The surgery was a success and I began the long road to recovery. During many of these long days, my mind would wander back to this person and I wondered if I would ever know anything about them this side of Heaven. I had written a letter to the family but in these situations the letter goes to the hospital and they deliver it. It was up to the family if those chose to respond. It took a year and a half but one day I got a letter. It was from Bonnie and she told me about her brother, Bill. She told me how happy she was that Bill's choice "could help someone else have life." It had been his choice. As she told me how he was an active member of his church, I fell to knees. She told me how he loved Jesus and I knew God had answered my prayer. Not only had God blessed me with another chance, he blessed me with the knowledge that he held the one who had given so much to me. She stated that she was so happy that Bill's work for the Lord was continuing and she knew he was in the presence of God. God is so good!!!!!

Then the analogy came to life. This individual had given his life and because of that I was given another chance at mine. I might not have ever known this individual, but because of this letter, I felt like I knew him personally. It all fit too well. For years I didn't realize the magnitude of Jesus' sacrifice. For years I didn't fully understand the price He had paid and the gift I had received. For years, I only knew Him as a figure on the Cross of the church wall but never as a personal Savior. That is until I read His letter, the Bible. I will never forget opening this love letter and reading about Him. Through these words I met Him and got to know Him personally. And through these words, my life was forever changed.

Maybe you've never experienced the miracle of being an organ transplant recipient. But you can experience the miracle of being a spirit transplant recipient. That's what Jesus does. He takes the old, decaying, dying part of us and replaces it with a new creation. And He did it by giving His life. Don't waste another day, another hour, another moment. Receive this gift if you never have. And if you have, renew this gift by re-reading his personal letter to you. It is the greatest gift you will ever receive, the gift of life!

❦ *Condition of the Heart* ❦

""Teacher, which is the most important commandment in the law of Moses?"

Jesus replied, "You must love the Lord your God with all your heart, all your

soul, and all your mind.' This is the first and greatest commandment. A

second is equally important: 'Love your neighbor as yourself.' The entire law

and all the demands of the prophets are based on these two

commandments.""

-Matthew 22:36-40 (NLT)

It is the middle of your last week on Earth. What do you do? Jesus knew what to do. He taught. He imparted. He shared. He spoke truth. He took this opportunity to teach about everything from money to hypocrisy. But in the middle of this concourse He gave the greatest truth, the one thing that if you missed everything else, this would revolutionize your life. He gave the commandment to love.

The thing that struck me as odd was that was delivered in the context of an order, something the people had to do. The strange thing was that how can you demand a genuine emotion. Anyone that has ever tried to make someone love them knows this is nearly impossible. True love is a condition of the heart. Then it hit me. He had to deliver the message in this manner because this was the mindset of the people. I saw this because right after that He really laid into the religious leaders of the day. If anyone should be keeping the commandments, it was them. But they were so far from keeping the greatest commandments: loving God and His people. It was a condition of the heart.

Then I read on and came to the place where Jesus is leaving the temple. He turns, looks back at the people, and He laments. I had to look that word up and it means that His heart ached because of His love for His children! Put yourself in that place. Desiring the love of your children but not getting it. How much that must hurt. But still having a love so strong that you are willing to do anything for your kids, even die.....

This is where Jesus was. Recently my wife wrote a comment on Face Book, "Always remind the ones that you love, that you love them. Not only by words, but by actions." This is what Jesus was doing. He loved His kids so much; He had to teach them right from wrong. Even when they were wrong. He loved them so much; He was willing to go that next step all the way to the cross. He loved them so much that He laid down His life to save theirs. I've heard it said that it wasn't the nails that held Him on the cross; it was His love for us. It was a condition of the heart.

As for the second commandment, any of us who have kids know the pain we feel when their relationship is damaged. In the end, Paul said it best in His letter to the Romans,

"Love does no wrong to anyone. That's why it fully satisfies all of God's

requirements. It is the only law you need."

Father, forgive me for when I haven't loved you the way I should. Thank you for having changed the condition of my heart for without You, I couldn't love. Help me to keep this love strong by staying close to you. Help me to love all those around me, even those that don't return it.

Lord, help us all as we remember your sacrifice this week. In your name we pray.
Amen.

To Know Him

"But whatever were gains to me I now consider loss for the sake of Christ. What is more, I consider everything a loss because of the surpassing worth of knowing Christ Jesus my Lord, for whose sake I have lost all things. I consider them garbage, that I may gain Christ and be found in him, not having a righteousness of my own that comes from the law, but that which is through faith in Christ—the righteousness that comes from God on the basis of faith. I want to know Christ...."

-Philippians 3:7-10 (NIV)

In the years we've been married, there's an important lesson my wife and I have learned. If we want our marriage to stay strong, we need to invest in it. In recent years we've seen too many relationships splinter and it has done something in us. These were long-time relationships of people who once had strong commitments to each other but somewhere along the way something happened and now what was once a united bond has become a broken union. I can't state the reason for each of these breakups but I have to believe in my heart that at some point they started spending less and less intimate time together and simply became roommates sharing a dwelling place but not a life. They changed and in the midst of that change

28

stopped knowing each other. One day they found themselves so far apart that the cord that had held them together simply broke and all those years dissolved. I'm determined to not allow this to be our fate!

So Saturday we invested. We got up early before the kids, packed a bag and simply headed out, just the two of us. No kids, no particular plans, just time. We started up the road and ended up in the foothills. First we stopped in Columbia, an old gold rush town. We then made our way up the hill to the snow. On the way we grabbed some lunch and found an isolated picnic table. We talked, we laughed, we prayed, we ate. We simply were continuing to get to know each other. It was such a wonderful day. In the midst of this day, our commitment to each other was strengthened. The strength needed to face the struggles of life was renewed and our union as one was refreshed. This was our way of making sure we were growing closer not apart. And all it took was time.

Isn't it the same with God? We can say we believe in our relationship with Him. We can voice our commitment to Him and have the external indications that this is the case but if we never invest in the relationship won't it end up just like the many broken marriages we see today? This scares me as much, if not more than losing my loving wife. I do not want to lose God!! And I will not lose my wife!! As I stated I've had 25 wonderful years with an incredible woman and 16 of those years have been incredible because Jesus joined the union. I refuse to lose the things that have made my life worth living. So I invest. And what's the best investment: Time. Whatever you invest your time in will flourish, whatever you don't invest your time in will dwindle. Don't let the relationships you've been blessed with dissolve. Invest....

Blessings.

"Then He said, "Go out, and stand on the mountain before the LORD."

And behold, the LORD passed by, and a great and strong wind tore into

the mountains and broke the rocks in pieces before the LORD, but the

LORD was not in the wind; and after the wind an earthquake, but the

LORD was not in the earthquake; and after the earthquake a fire, but the

LORD was not in the fire; and after the fire a still small voice."

-1 Kings 19:11-12 (NKJV)

Everyday on my way to work I cross over the Stanislaus River and everyday I would wonder where the trails down below lead. But, until one fine special day, that's all it was, a thought. I happened to be heading down the same road, crossing the same bridge with my son and I decided to stop wondering and actually go down and check it out.

When we went down what we found was amazing. At the onset of the trail, we saw squirrels running in every direction. My son called me over and pointed out an ant hill with some of the biggest red ants either one of us had ever seen. As we approached the river, there was a bridge to walk across and in the middle of the bridge we both simply stopped and listened. Even though the sounds of the nearby freeway were still present, they somehow were muffled by the stillness of this new found world. Birds were chirping, butterflies were fluttering, and small animals were scattering in the brush. I looked and I was sure I saw a fish lazily swimming by and I realized how there was this whole new world existing in my path every day. I also realized that I could have kept going to work everyday for years, always

31

wondering about this place but never experiencing its beauty and peace. What a loss that would have been!

Isn't that how our life with God can be? We live in this world that demands so much from us that we can daily pass by God and wonder what life with Him is like but never stop to appreciate this life. Sunday during our worship service, our song leader stopped the music and the church got so quiet you could here a pin drop. Suddenly I was taken back to that place on the bridge and I heard that still small voice again. And you know what it said? Peace. In the midst of this life there is peace in His stillness. Comfort and security that surpasses the hustle and bustle of this world. The only problem, you have to slow down to hear it.

My Friends, never let this life rob you of this peace. If you've never experienced it, find that quiet place and listen for that still small voice and I promise you that if you seek it He won't let you down. After all, like that Eagle's song says, "Life in the fast lane will surely make you lose your mind."

Lord, help us all to slow down and hear that still small voice that leads to your peace. Help us to fight against the busyness of this life that robs us of our true spiritual life with you. Thank you for continuing to speak in the midst and never tiring of our lack of listening. Today, help us to hear you and today we will thank you!

Be blessed!

To All the Girls
I've Loved Before

"Love is patient and kind; love does not envy or boast; it is not arrogant or rude.

It does not insist on its own way; it is not irritable or resentful; it does not rejoice at

wrongdoing, but rejoices with the truth. Love bears all things, believes all things,

hopes all things, endures all things. Love never ends."

-1 Corinthians 13:4-7 (ESV)

I can only imagine the look on my wife's face as she reads this title but I have to admit it, while she is my greatest love, there have been others......

I will never forget the first time I saw this girl. It was as if all other things suddenly melted away and she was the center of the universe. Her innocent beauty was so stunning it literally took my breath away and it was love at first sight! This encounter was so moving and unforgettable that I remember not sleeping that night. I will never forget the next morning's sunrise. I was sure it was the greatest sunrise ever and I knew that a new day in my life had begun. Life itself was never the same after that and I am still feeling the impact of this girl today. As this relationship continued to grow, this beautiful young woman continued to grow. She had her moments and was definitely headstrong at times but she was always as inspiring as she was strong. I watched her as she blossomed into this amazing woman who I knew could do anything she set

33

her mind to. I am so thankful that she came into my life because a lot of who I am is because of her....

The next girl came as a bit of surprise. But I've got to say it was one of those wonderful surprises! She was such an opposite of the first girl I spoke of but hers was also a radiant beauty. When I first saw her face it just seemed to shine with such a special joy and it continues to do so to this day. She was my mischievous one and her antics make for some of the greatest memories and smiles of the day. She was also the fearless one, never afraid to do anything. If there was a dare she wouldn't back down and if there was a moment to stretch the limits, you could count on her to do that. While sometimes this wasn't always the wisest of choices, it was always the greatest of spirits. In this I knew she would go far and to this day I know she will. Her personality is one of a kind and her spunk is phenomenal. I have also watched her transform into a beautiful woman who has filled my heart so deeply words cannot describe the feelings....

Years separated the next one but her impact was not diminished. She came into my life during a turbulent time but brought hope back to me. She had the cutest of faces and the warmest of smiles. It's funny though, she also had the strongest of lungs and could be heard when she wanted to be. Things didn't always come easy to her but she never gave up. In her I learned the meaning of determination and when things didn't come easy, she simply pressed in. Her beauty was there from the beginning and only grew as she came into her own. She was definitely independent and continues to impress me with her frugalness which could not be seen by her style. She is herself and worries not about others but carries herself with her head held high. She doesn't doubt she can do anything and this spirit is contagious. She has divided my heart as well and entered in with a portion that will always be only hers....

Finally there is my first love. Ours was a troubled relationship. The beginning was that of a true love story of sacrifice. She took me in when no one else would and opened her heart to a lost soul and for this I will be forever in her debt. But it is not a debt that is owed but a love that can never be repaid nor should it be tried to. The earliest of memories are those of true happiness and even though those times didn't last, those moments drive me to the example that was set. She held me and holds me like no other woman ever will. Her beauty was so exquisite it carries itself deep into my being and imprints itself on my soul. She went through some very difficult times but continued to do the best she could with what she had. And every time I saw her, I knew there was a love so strong there for me that it burned itself into my very existence. She began the work of molding me and her efforts live on to this day. There will always be something so special about this first love and words still struggle to paint this picture. But hearts who have experienced it will know what I speak of.....

I can't go on any longer without naming all of these special women. First there was Jessica, then Yvette and Ariel. When God looked down and blessed me with these three beautiful daughters my heart grew. It had to in order to fit in all the love and joy they brought into my life. They have all become the most incredible women a man could ever ask for and I am so proud to call all of them my daughters. They are a part of me that will live on and I know that they themselves will impact this world. Thank you Lord for these treasures!!

Then there is my first love, my mom.
Like I had mentioned, ours was a troubled relationship. But you know what, there is something to be said about troubled relationships when they are restored like ours was. For this I am eternally grateful to God. Because of Him, we got through the difficult times and moved on. In this I knew that her love for me had never faltered. I also learned of forgiveness and longsuffering. She was a woman who did go through so much that I am sure her joy in Heaven is far greater than her sufferings on this Earth. Thank you Lord for her! She was perfect and I am a product of her. Hold her tightly for me until we meet again.....

Men, be blessed by the women you have in your life. They are the true gems of existence. I've learned this from experience. I take back every time I asked why I had to live with a houseful of ladies, because now I know, these ladies made me who I am today.
Eternally blessed!!!

༺〰༻ *To Be Real* ༺〰༻

"Not all those who say 'You are our Lord' will enter the kingdom of heaven.

The only people who will enter the kingdom of heaven are those who do what

my Father in heaven wants. On the last day many people will say to me, 'Lord,

Lord, we spoke for you, and through you we forced out demons and did many

miracles.' Then I will tell them clearly, 'Get away from me, you who do evil. I

never knew you.'"

-Matthew 7:21-23 (NCV)

In the last 15 years that I've been walking with Lord I must say that I've learned a lot. I've learned how to walk this "Christian walk."
I've learned how to talk this "Christian talk." I've learned when to say hallelujah and amen, "God bless you" and "In Jesus Name." In fact, I've learned so much that I could fool even the most pious of Christians into believing that I was truly walking close as close can be to God. But the greatest of lessons: I can't fool God!

Maybe I do wake up every morning and read my daily devotion. Maybe I do listen to a different preacher talk about God on the way to work.
Maybe I do have my radio station tuned in to the local Christian station and have a library full of the latest Christian books. Sure enough you can catch me in Church every Wednesday, Friday AND Sunday.
All of these things must mean I've got this Christian thing down. And they do. I got this!! Problem is....in the midst of all this.....where's God?

In the last seven days I've seen seven wonderful things revealed to me. But this devotion is not about that path, it's about this wonderful conclusion:
I need Jesus!

I don't need to hear others talk about Jesus, or read about Jesus, or sing a song about Jesus. I NEED JESUS!!

Don't get me wrong. All of these things are wonderful vessels pointing towards the destination; they're just not the destination. He's the destination. He's the Way, the Truth, and the Light. Without Him, all the other things are merely religious shells making me feel good about myself for the moment but doing nothing for my soul. Bottom line: I'm tired of playing church. I'm tired of playing "Christian". I'm tired of fooling myself.

You know what I've learned in these 15 years: I don't have all the answers. I don't always know what to do or say. But I do know a God who does. Moral to the story: Let go and let God!! (Deep revelations come with simple answers). Will you join me on this quest?

Lord,
Today I truly feel you brought these words out of my heart. Forgive us for letting our "religious" duties replace the only thing that really matters-time spent with you. Forgive us if we allow our routine to replace our relationship. Bring us back to that intimate place with you and show us that in this place, everything we do is an act of worship. Only here will we achieve true peace and happiness. Thank you for your never-ending grace and mercy. Today we commit to you.
In Jesus name,
Amen

"When he was still a long way off, his father saw him. His heart pounding, he

ran out, embraced him, and kissed him."

-Luke 15:20b (MSG)

Vacation is refreshing but there is something to be said about coming home and getting back to that familiar place and that sense of security and belonging, knowing that you've arrived at your "castle."

On a recent trip, my son and I have shared this moment but what makes the moment even grander is the anticipation of it. When we awoke to head home, he jumped up with a joy and a smile and in an excited voice exclaimed, "Dad, we're going home!!" You know it really wasn't about the place we were returning to but the people. It was about getting back into the presence of the ones we loved and feeling their embrace.

I am a blessed man because my wife has this wonderful way of making us feel so special when we arrive. The way she runs out with an unmistakable excitement and true sense of joy at the very sight of us is simply amazing.

But you know the funny thing, I don't only get that emotion when I return from a week long journey. I get it every day when I return from a day at work. Every day when I leave, I call to let her know I'm coming and every day I'm greeted with that same joy. The great thing is it doesn't matter if I'm late or if the morning was bad or whatever the circumstance. She is always glad that we are about to be reunited again. I can't begin to tell you how special this makes me feel. I truly love this about my wife!!

Then the thought came: What about God? As I reflected on my earthly experiences, I realized that I had a Father in Heaven who was waiting with the same excitement and anticipation of the day that we would be reunited. I began to think of that homecoming and what a celebration it would be. How He told me in His Word that Heaven rejoices at the arrival of His Saints and that I was counted among them. This revelation lifted my love for Him up a level. In my wife I saw how He felt about me and for this I am truly grateful.

Lord,
Thank you for this vision. We thank you for these homecomings here on earth and the embrace of loved ones but let us not lose sight of the fact that this is only a temporary home. Put in our hearts that same anticipation that you have in yours of a wonderful reunion. Help us to display these characteristics of you so that others may see the shadows of the wonderful things to come and we will truly be a blessed people here on Earth as well as in Heaven.
Amen.

❦ *The Value of Hairspray* ❦

"Love each other with genuine affection, and take delight in honoring

each other."

-Romans 12:10 (NLT)

In the not too distant past, my wife and I were excited about a trip we were taking to Nashville. I had gotten about a mile up the road when suddenly she let out an exasperating gasp and exclaimed, "My hairspray, I forgot it!" We were running late, had a plane to catch and I didn't know if we were going to hit traffic on the way to the airport so in my mind I thought, "big deal, we can get hairspray anywhere." I got frustrated and said, with a terrible attitude I'm sure, "Do you want me to go back?" She looked at me and put her head down and of course said no, let's just go. The rest of the trip was pretty silent. As I was driving, God quickened me. What was so important about this hairspray that upset her so? After all, in my thinking it couldn't have cost more than a few dollars, but that wasn't it. It wasn't really about the hairspray. It was about my lack of sensitivity to something that was of value to my wife. She had a particular brand she enjoyed using and we were going to an important banquet and now she was going to have to use something she wasn't familiar with. It was about valuing my wife and honoring the things that are important to her. So the value of that hairspray was much more than a few dollars, it was priceless. After all, had it been my special cologne........

This has made me think and pray for a new spirit and a new attitude for those around me, especially my family. We can get so comfortable in our ways with those closest to us that we don't realize that we are taking them for granted. My wife and I have been together for years and I can't imagine life without her but at the same time, I don't always show that. I say it but let's face it, actions speak louder than words. Five minutes invested into turning around and getting the thing that was important to her would have shown my respect for her thoughts and feelings. Even missing the plane would have been worth honoring my wife. At that moment I prayed, "Lord, help me to be sensitive to her and others around me when they speak of things that are important to them, regardless of how I feel. Let me see their true value!"

I shared this story with a man who had recently lost his wife. She had a certain shampoo which she used and he did something similar in not respecting that. He told me how he wished he could have those moments again when she would get angry with him. How he would go and get her that special brand no matter the time of day or the cost......but he couldn't. Of course that hit home. I know many of us have lost loved ones and there are things we wish we could go back and do differently. I also know that in these circumstances, our loved ones know and knew of our love for them, as I stated to this gentlemen. He agreed but he also said it changed how he interacts with those around him now. I thanked him, then I prayed,

"Lord,

Help us to be sensitive to the people you've placed in our lives. Whether it be our spouses, children, family members, friends, co-workers, or even strangers that we meet, let us have eyes that see things through their perspective and not ours. Let us value their needs, their thoughts, their hurts, and their "hairsprays." Let us never again take for granted the wonderful blessing of people we are surrounded with. Thank you for each and every one. And thank you for loving us and valuing our lives so much you gave your life for us. Thank you for always hearing our prayers, regardless of their content, and always valuing them!"

Be blessed today by those around you!

This Is the Big One

"And we know that God causes everything to work together for the good

of those who love God and are called according to his purpose for them."

-Romans 8:28 (NLT)

One of my favorite shows growing up was Sanford and Son. Fred Sanford (Redd Foxx) was such a character and his antics always had me rolling. He was always coming up with a get rich quick scheme and his "charisma" was too much. Whether it was his dealings with his son (you "big dummy") or his put downs of Esther and her quick responses ("Watch it Sucka!), the show was hilarious. But some of my favorite scenes were the faked heart attacks. Fred would stumble back, reach for his heart and start the famous line, "This is it, this is the big one....Elizabeth, I'm comin' to join ya..."
Those heart attacks always came at the perfect moment, for Fred that is, and they were "The Big Ones." Too funny. But sometimes, sometimes, in life we can find ourselves in Fred's shoes, only our situations aren't faked and our "attacks" can truly feel like the big one. Only our line is "This is it, this is the big one.....God, I'm comin' to join ya....there's no way I can live through this one!!"

Ever had one of those? I've got to say that I've had a couple. They don't come often. And they're not the everyday trials that I'm speaking of. They're "The Big Ones." The ones where you find yourself in a situation or circumstance and you have no idea how God or anyone can ever help you through this. Everything around you turns dark in that moment and you don't understand it. Too often everything was going great just yesterday and suddenly today is disaster. Sometimes we see it coming but we try to pretend it will never arrive, like a far off storm where you can see the clouds but somehow you hope the winds of life will blow it away. It can involve loss. A loved one, a job, a home. Health, finances, relationship. It can hit you personally or it can hit someone so close to you that it might as well have hit you personally. No matter how it comes, it hits with force and such impact that it causes us all to question the future and what it has in store for us. But, with all that said, it also comes with some hidden treasures. Some prizes that unfortunately can only be obtained by traversing this course I speak of and seeing it through. Not by your strength but by strength that is beyond ourselves. In the midst of that, these "Big Ones" come with the greatest of blessings, the ability to know that there is hope in every situation faced and strength to arrive at the other side.

The first time I had to face a giant like this it had to do with my health. Receiving bad news in this area can be devastating. Finding out that our mortality is threatened throws everything in a tail spin. The past is regretted and the future is lost. But something happened to me in this circumstance that can never be taken away from me. I made it through. It's really that simple but the fact of the matter is in the moment I couldn't see myself overcoming and I knew that I didn't have the strength to fight this fight. In retrospect, I realize that since I couldn't see the finish line and since I lacked strength, I was left with only one other weapon, faith. This is the tool that produces that great blessing of hope. But I must say that when you're in you're very first "Big One," your faith is still the size of that mustard seed. Everyone around you is telling you to have it and you know you should lean on it, but the reality is that if you haven't personally experienced it, it's still a seed and it's hard to lean on seeds. But then something begins to happen. That seed sprouts and suddenly a tender young plant emerges. You see its first signs of life and you start to consider it. Something sparks and you come back to visit it more often. The next time you notice that the stock is just a bit stronger and there are some branches developing. Another visit brings a little more height to it and the leaves you see bring it depth. Suddenly you realize that these frequent visits to this small seed have produce a strong plant that is able to withstand the elements and you realize that something is different, something has been birthed inside, and at the end of that "Big One" you know, "*All things work together for good.....*" But let's not forget the rest of the verse, "*for those who love God....*"

I wish I could tell that this was a magic formula that allows you to face everything in life without pain and always smiling. It's not. I wish I could tell you that this means that if you love God bad things won't happen in your life. It doesn't. But I can tell you this. This seed, if allowed to grow to the strong plant it's intended to be, can develop such deep roots that even when the huge storms of life come, we are so deeply anchored that we know that no matter what, it will be okay. Will doubts come? Yes. Can they stay? No. Why? Because now you've lived it. You've lived the verse above. They're not just words being told you by people that you know you should listen to but not sure how. They're whispers from a Father you trust who you've seen in action and know He has the wisdom and strength to see you through. Suddenly, deep felt peace settles in. Storms will come, but you know, that they will also go. And in the morning....the Son/Sun will shine again.

If you find yourself for the first time in one of these "Big Ones," remember the seed and visit it daily and watch it grow. If you find yourself back in another "Big One," anchor onto the roots. In either case, be thankful, for "all things work together for the good for those who love God and are called according to His purpose."

Today, love God and be blessed.

⁓⁓ *Beauty for Ashes* ⁓⁓

"The Spirit of the Sovereign LORD is upon me, because the LORD has

appointed me to bring good news to the poor. He has sent me to comfort

the brokenhearted and to announce that captives will be released and

prisoners will be freed....

....To all who mourn in Israel, he will give beauty for ashes, joy instead of

mourning, praise instead of despair. For the LORD has planted them like

strong and graceful oaks for his own glory."

-Isaiah 61:1-:3 (NLT)

I've come to the conclusion that tears are truly a
blessing from God. It was confirmed last night when
I turned to my wife at church and watched them
streaming down her cheek. Granted there are
different types of tears but these were Godly drops.
These were, "I'm in God's presence" tears and when
you're in that place there's nothing more that you
can do but cry. When you're really there, all of a
sudden there's a realization of how unworthy of this
place you are and how great God is. But you know
what really makes the tears flow? In this place you
are face-to-face with the greatest force on Earth:
Love. But not just any love, God's love. It's
overwhelming. It's unconditional. He knows you. He
knows your faults; your weaknesses; your mistakes.
He knows....and He loves.

Suddenly you realize that this kind of love is yours
but many times you haven't acknowledged it;
haven't lived as if it mattered, as if it even existed at
times. And the pain comes. But, because God is who
He is, it doesn't stop there. He lets the tears fall
because they have a purpose. It's the reason He

48

created them. In the natural a tears purpose is to cleanse the eye. In the spiritual it's to cleanse the soul; to wash away the hurt and pain and replace it with the love. And there it is, the Blessing.

So the next time those tears begin to fall, follow them into His presence and remember His Word:

"Distress that drives us to God does that. It turns us around. It gets us back in the way of salvation. We never regret that kind of pain. But those who let distress drive them away from God are full of regrets, end up on a deathbed of regrets."

-2 Corinthians 7:10 (MSG)

And:

"Those who plant in tears will harvest with shouts of joy. They weep as they go to plant their seed, but they sing as they return with the harvest."

-Psalms 126:5-6 (NLT)

But, even more importantly, know that not a tear is lost or in vain:

"You keep track of all my sorrows. You have collected all my tears in your bottle. You have recorded each one in your book."

-Psalm 56:8 (NLT)

Thank you Lord for your Love and for remembering my every hurt and tear.
Amen.

Today, Be blessed!

"Haven't you read the Scriptures?" Jesus replied. "They record that from the beginning 'God made them male and female. And he said, 'This explains why a man leaves his father and mother and is joined to his wife, and the two are united into one. Since they are no longer two but one, let no one split apart what God has joined together."

-Matthew 19:4-6 (NLT)

It is six in the morning and I'm sitting on my porch with my eyes fixated on the house across the street and my memory going back to times more that a quarter of a century ago. It's funny that I still live in the same house more than 25 years later......and it's even funnier that the woman who lives with me lives across the street from the house of her youth more than 25 years later. Obviously we haven't gone far in terms of geography. But we have gone far in other areas......

All of a sudden I'm wondering what it must have been like for her father as he watched his beautiful, young, innocent little girl begin to have emotions for the boy across the street. Did he know of the times she would sneak out and be so close to home but yet in another world? I do know that the more he became aware, the less he liked it and I can't blame him. You see there were quite a few "social gatherings" at my house and let's just say it wasn't the church group coming over for Bible Study in those days ☺. I can only imagine the conversations that went on between a father and his daughter about the perils of life, boys, and did he even go there…..sex?!?!? That's a tough one to talk to your 16 year old daughter about. Maybe he should've of looking back but would it have made a difference? I don't know but we all know it's better than not talking about it in the days we live in. But in the end, as this Scripture says, she left her father and immersed herself into the wonderful institution God created: Marriage. And the blessing, nothing has split apart what God joined together more than 25 years ago! Funny thing, for the first time in my life I can appreciate what he must have went through.

So as I sit here on this porch and prepare to watch one of my little girls follow the love of her life into this God-ordained institution I have mixed emotions. First I can't believe how time has past. Where did it go? Then I still struggle with the fact that she will be calling another man instead of me in times of trouble. Then I'm thankful because she's found such a wonderful young man who I trust and admire. Then I go back to the first thought. Then…….the thought…..I have two more girls that I have to go through this all over again and again…..

Then I realize, while all the worries and concerns of my wife's father were legitimate, we came out alright. In fact we came out more than alright, we came out blessed! And I've got to say that a part of the reason that we came out blessed was because my father-in-law taught his daughter well. He instilled in her a character that shines through to this day. And the things that her earthly father couldn't do, her Heavenly Father stepped in and took care. And the result: a warm, loving, wonderful family that has had its shares of struggles but has grown stronger and closer through each and every one of them. And the bond, even when we didn't know it, has always been God.

So the moral to the story, I feel good this morning. I believe I have raised three amazing young woman and a phenomenal son and as each of them has begun their own journey, I know that they will be alright. I have done what I could do and what I couldn't, God picked up. They have known me, and they have known their Heavenly Father. They have a Godly mother who has taught them what it is to be a woman. And in spite of all my fears, they will be okay. So this morning I thank God for this moment of reflection. I pray that it inspire you to love those around you even a little bit more if that is at all possible. Show them yourself, and instill the bond that has made this family what it is. Never perfect, but always secure in the Love of God!! This has been our secret to success, let it be yours too...you will never go wrong.

Today, be blessed!
I know I am......

﹌ *Be Blessed* ﹌

"Enter a place where you never have to cry Never have to live a lie, never have to wonder why Never want for nothing you're always satisfied In the peace that his arms will provide He will erase any guilt or shame, any bad habits you've got You won't wanna do em again, Yes we all can change, I can testify See I spoke to God, I called out your name And on your behalf, I just asked, If he would be there for you I want you to....

....Be Blessed, Don't live life in distress Just let go, let God, He'll work it out for you I pray that your soul will be blessed Forever in his rest, Cause you deserve his best no less."

-"Be Blessed" by Yolanda Adams

I love this song and just had to share a piece of its lyrics. In fact, there are a lot of times that I use those two powerful words, "Be blessed!" But what does that mean? How do you "Be blessed"?

I feel that I've gone on a journey with these words. Early on being blessed had to do with escaping the hurts and pains that this life had brought. Broken home, troubled marriage, bad habits, all I wanted was life restored. And when this happened I was blessed! And this was an important part of the meaning of those words, but not all.

Then I started to look towards career, better car, nicer house, more money, and when these things started to materialize then for sure I knew I was blessed. And these were good things but there had to be more to it.

Suddenly, due to an illness, the bottom fell out and I had to rethink my definition of these words. Now the money was funny, the career was in jeopardy, and the material things didn't seem so important. I had to ask myself, was I still blessed? And it was here that the answer came.

I'll never forget a night I spent alone with the Lord questioning Him as to why this was happening to me now. After all, I had turned my life around. I was in ministry and in church at least three times a week, I went back to school and earned a college degree, I had made a good name in my career and was on the road to success......why now?!?!?

Suddenly, out of nowhere, He spoke to my heart. First, all of those things that "I" had done were accomplished because of Him. And even if I never "accomplished" another thing, I WAS a blessed man! Second, at the beginning all I had asked for was restoration of a broken life and I had got that. I WAS a blessed man! Finally, the clincher, God had never promised me that life would not have its problems. He only promised that He would never leave me alone through those difficult times. And He hasn't. I AM A BLESSED MAN!!!

Being blessed isn't about possessions or material things. Being blessed isn't about living a problem free life (If this were the case there wouldn't be a blessed person on this Earth). Being blessed has nothing to do with me. It's all about Him. It's an attitude, a mindset, a way of life. It's knowing that you are a child of a loving Father who will never leave you or forsake you. It's understanding and being confident that no matter what happens in this life, it's going to be alright.

It's faith in our Savior. That is how to "Be blessed!" Not always easy, but if you hang on to it, it can never be taken away.

As evidenced by this writing, God restored me again. Possibly to share this thought with you today. Yolanda Adams finished the song well:

"My prayer for you today, Is that you trust and always obey. On this day keep calling. On this day keep calling. He'll keep you from falling. He'll keep you from falling. He'll supply the answers. Yes He will, if you stand in faith and trust Him to make a way out of no way."

Today, Be Blessed!

(Be Blessed by Yolanda Adams)

༄ ⌇⌇⌇ *Clothe Yourself* ༄ ⌇⌇⌇

"Since God chose you to be the holy people he loves, you must clothe yourselves

with tenderhearted mercy, kindness, humility, gentleness, and patience. Make

allowance for each other's faults, and forgive anyone who offends you.

Remember, the Lord forgave you, so you must forgive others. Above all, clothe

yourselves with love, which binds us all together in perfect harmony. And let

the peace that comes from Christ rule in your hearts. For as members of one

body you are called to live in peace. And always be thankful."

-Colossians 3:12-15 (NLT)

My wife and I had a memorable moment on a recent
sightseeing trip. We found ourselves with a day where
all the kids had plans and were going in different
directions. No one was left in the house but her and I
on a bright and beautiful Saturday morning. We both
immediately decided to take advantage of this
opportunity and take a road trip. Since it was a spur of
the moment decision, San Francisco became our target
since it's not too far from our home and off we went.

My wife had been wanting to try Chicken and Waffles
and we had heard of a great place, Gussie's, in the
Fillmore District so this was our prime destination. But
since we had all day to spare, we also had heard of a
hidden away spot called China Beach so this is where we
started our adventure. I must say that this spot was
beautiful! It sat on the far side of the Golden Gate with
the ocean on one side and the Bay on the other.
Magnificent. Being one never to settle down, I saw that
we were close to the Bridge and a local told us of
another spot nearby, Baker Beach, so off we went. This
spot was not quite as secluded and much more
populated but it had sights of its own. One of which we

were not expecting. As we were walking we decided to take this mile hike trail which led to the Golden Gate. Everything was going great until suddenly I heard a gasp from wife. As we approached a corner of the beach we were shocked to see a pair of 60+ year old men naked!! Let's just say that this wasn't the sight either of us were looking to see!! I have to admit that I couldn't help but chuckle a bit but at the same time the thought came, you really need to go and clothe yourself!! It wasn't a pretty sight……

Then the next day God brings me this Scripture, "you must clothe yourselves with tenderhearted mercy, kindness, humility, gentleness, and patience." I started contemplating and I realized that sometimes these things don't come easily and that I have to make a physical effort to put these things on, kindness, mercy, gentleness, and patience. Sometimes people face me who I must say incline me to put on a different wardrobe of frustration, anger, or bitterness. Sometimes situations face me that make me want to put on despair, hopelessness, and anxiety. Sometimes I don't want to put on anything at all (in a spiritual sense) and simply crawl into my bed and not face the day to come.

But then I'm reminded, above all, I must clothe myself in love. Love for the people around me, love for the life I've been given regardless of the situations, and love for the God who promises to be with me even in the time of utter despair and hopelessness. I am reminded that there is no situation without hope, regardless of mistakes made and adversities confronted. And I'm reminded that no matter what I am forgiven and loved. These Scriptures are more than words. They are a love letter from a Father who cares about his children. They are a reminder that whatever I/we are facing, we are not alone. And above all, they are a reminder that love is present.

Sometimes clothing myself in this sense may be a little more difficult than the men on the beach who simply needed some swimming trunks, but the only other option is to go out into the world naked and this is not a way I will choose to face my days. I will clothe myself with love and Christ and press in to whatever the day has to offer.

Today, clothe yourself and be blessed.

❧ *Live, Love, Laugh* ❧

This morning I awaken ready to start a new week, a
new day. And I am expecting new things. What has
happened in the past is past. A time of reflection has
released freshness. And it can all be summed up in the
popular saying. "Live, Love, Laugh."

Live

"The thief's purpose is to steal and kill and destroy. My purpose is to give them

a rich and satisfying life."

-John 10:10 (NLT)

I have had enough of life stolen from me in the past.
Whether it was by bad decisions, circumstances or
simply my own procrastination, the reality is that I only
have one life to live. And that life is made up of today.
Today and many more today's stringed carefully
together which very quickly become a lifetime. I am
committed not to allow this string of events become a
lifetime of regrets but instead a memory of satisfaction.
A satisfaction that life was lived to the fullest. I was
created to live a rich and satisfying life. I have been
given the ability to live such a life. And too often, it is
only I that stands in the way of achieving this forward
progress. I will get out of the way and press on!

Love

"Three things will last forever—faith, hope, and love—and the greatest of

these is love."

-1 Corinthians 13:13

Love is what it all boils down to. It is the greatest of commandments. It is the greatest of forces in the world. From it true faith rises. From it true hope appears. And from it, the world is seen through different lenses.

"Love is patient and kind. Love is not jealous or boastful or proud or rude. It

does not demand its own way. It is not irritable, and it keeps no record of

being wronged. It does not rejoice about injustice but rejoices whenever the

truth wins out. Love never gives up, never loses faith, is always hopeful, and

endures through every circumstance"

-1 Corinthians 13:4-7 (NLT)

I will love. I will love my wife. I will love my children. I will love my family. I will love my friends. I will love my co-workers, my acquaintances, my encounters. I will love my enemies. I will love mankind. Why? Because I am loved. Because I am loved I know what it is to love even in the midst of mistakes. Why? Because I make mistakes. It is not emotion I speak of, it is committed action. Action which will only occur by the greatest driving force in the world: Love. I will love!

Laugh

"A joyful heart is good medicine,

But a broken spirit dries up the bones."

-Proverbs 17:22 (ESV)

I will laugh. It is the greatest of medicines, the purest of treatments. It makes the difference in the disposition of life. It reminds us that there is hope. It brings true joy. And it is contagious. It is an outward manifestation of an inward accomplishment. A peace within that knows that life is to be enjoyed. It is to be enwrapped, engulfed. It is to be taken in, good and bad, and always brought back to the center of its existence, a joy for the very gift of it. I will laugh for laughter produces a smile. And the force of a smile is undeniable. Walk through a crowded room and make that eye contact that reflects the peace within by the smile on the outside. I will be that smile. I will bring happiness to a room not despair. I will bring lightness of spirit not heaviness of heart. I will love life and you will know. Why? Because I will laugh!

Today my friends, I will live, love and laugh.
No matter what the circumstance. Why? Because I know there is always hope at the end.

Today, join me in this quest. Together, we will make our world a better place.
Today, be blessed.

❧ *I Know Him* ❧

"The LORD is my shepherd;

I shall not want.

He makes me to lie down in green pastures;

He leads me beside the still waters.

He restores my soul;

He leads me in the paths of righteousness

For His name's sake.

Yea, though I walk through the valley of the shadow of death,

I will fear no evil;

For You are with me;

Your rod and Your staff, they comfort me.

You prepare a table before me in the presence of my enemies;

You anoint my head with oil;

My cup runs over.

Surely goodness and mercy shall follow me

All the days of my life;

And I will dwell in the house of the LORD

Forever."

-Psalm 23 (NKJV)

This summer I've been blessed with watching something develop before my eyes and last night God showed it to me clearly. This summer my son had the opportunity to work with his Grandparents. They are gardeners at heart and feel the most at peace when they are working in God's creation. Well, when the opportunity presented itself, I can honestly say that there were two benefits that I thought my son would gain from this.

First one: money. He is a young teenage boy and it's time he start to learn how to handle finances and what better way to ease him in than a part-time summer job. Plus it eases the, "Dad, can I have this; Dad can I have that" syndrome. Now if he wants "it" he can save and purchase himself, hence financial responsibility.

Second was work ethic. I have to say that my son is a typical 14 year old. When it comes to the chores around the house, it can be a job just getting him to do his job sometimes. Now don't get me wrong, he's a good boy and occasionally......he'll surprise us and do everything he's supposed to without being asked but usually I'm sure there are much more important things that occupy the mind of a 14 year old boy. But this summer something in him changed, suddenly he started wanting to go to work. He gained responsibility of duty and I have to say that I was very proud of him. In fact, one day I wanted to do something with him and he told me, "Dad, Grandma needs me on Mondays." Aaahhh, my son is growing up and I am a proud dad!

But not until yesterday did I see the true value of this summer. My wife had gone to my parent's house and I had to go to the store so my son had the choice of going with either one of us. He wanted to go to his grandparents. I didn't think much of it until I got home and realized I also had to go talk to my dad so I called to let him know I was coming. Before I left my wife got home but she was alone. I asked her, "Where's Isaac?" and she said he wanted to stay at his grandparent's house. I still didn't see the significance until I got there myself and then the Lord spoke to me. My son was there sitting in the living room simply spending time with the ones he loves. It hit me: my son had developed relationship with his grandparents!!

This may sound funny because you may say, well hasn't he known them his whole life and yes he has. You might say haven't they always been around and yes they have. But just having someone around does not constitute the building of relationship. Relationship only comes when time is spent getting to know that person. This summer my son not only worked, he spent time getting to know his grandparents even better and now they are even closer than they have ever been before. Now this bond is strengthened and my son is blessed by a stronger relationship with people who truly love him and will be there for him no matter what. And all it took was time.

And of course this where God shifted the light to my relationship with Him. This morning I was lead to Psalm 23 and God had me read it again. I saw how this is one of the most popular verses in the Bible and millions have memorized it but how many actually live it? Stop and read it again, *"The Lord is my Shepherd...."* He's mine....and I'm his. We are close. He leads me. I follow. He comforts me. He holds me when I'm afraid. And He will guide me home to His house. None of this is possible without relationship. Reading this daily will not bring the reality these words hold to life, only a true relationship will. A relationship that is so embedded in the heart that the truth and faith in this bond causes the words to be solemn promises. A relationship that has sunk in and become a way of life knowing that we are loved and that He will be there for us no matter what. And all it takes for a relationship like this....TIME.

This morning if you have taken the time to read this I am blessed and you have come to know me a little bit more. But today if you take the time to know Him, **you** will be blessed and suddenly you will be able to truly say, "I will fear no evil because **You are with me**....."

Today, take the time and be blessed.

In Honor Of

"Every time I think of you, I give thanks to my God."

-Philippians 1:3 (NLT)

Life is full of heroes. There are those ones we read about who risk their lives for others and do things that make us awe at their courage; the passerby who pulls someone from a burning car or a raging river; the fireman who enters the flames and comes out with someone's beloved, the policeman who stops a tragedy. Then there are those whose acts of kindness and sacrifice make us marvel. The Mother Theresa's who give their lives for the poor. The Martin Luther King's who stand for justice even at the cost of their own lives. Then there are the heroes who live amongst us; the ones who God has placed in our midst whom we must not forget. Last week I got to know one of those heroes.

Her name was Faye. If you would have passed Faye on the street you probably wouldn't have recognized her. You never read about her in the local paper. She didn't stand out much to society. But that is where society missed out because to those whom she touched, they knew. They knew what a true hero this woman was and as I was honored to speak and listen at her memorial service to celebrate her life, I got to know too.

Let me start by saying its funny how these heroes are sometimes in our midst and we miss it. That is what happened with me and Faye. Faye was the mother to my daughter's, in-law's, husband (I think I got that right). We had shared holiday meals and sat at the same parties. But I missed her magnitude until last Friday. As I sat and listened I began to hear of this woman who, as a young lady, broke her high school record in the 50 yard dash. I learned how she had taken younger cousins and nieces and nurtured them. In fact, as her niece spoke, I saw what an influence in lives she had been. She loved to socialize and she was always the last one to leave the party. If you needed to laugh, she had a way. Whether singing was your thing or not, she drew the karaoke out of those around her, even though she couldn't carry a note. I was told that she had given so much of her life to those around her that the certificates of gratitude for her volunteer work no longer fit on wall that was set aside to house them. I could go on and on. Even though I didn't personally experience these things, by the end of that day, I felt that I had been blessed with living amongst a hero.

But I must say that the greatest evidence of this was found in her son. As her son got up and spoke, we all knew that he had been her greatest life's work. And what a job she had done. If you knew this man, you would know what I mean. He has become a modern day warrior. He served our country as a Marine. He serves our society as an Officer. And he gives back to our community as a martial arts teacher to under-privileged children at a local church. He stands strong with humility and, in his own words, he owes it all to the one who showed him what it is to stand strong in the midst of adversity, his mother Faye.

Is there a hero like this who has crossed your path? It could be your parent, your spouse, a child, a son-in-law, a peer, co-worker, or friend. Whoever it is, stop today and acknowledge them. Maybe they're no longer with us. Today is a good day to give thanks to God for the time that they were. Maybe they're in your midst. Today is a good day to let them know how much you appreciate them. Whatever the circumstance, let us be blessed by the heroes God has given us.

At the end of this Celebration of Life, I was honored to close in prayer. As I looked out at the audience I marveled at what I saw. The room was full with a diversity of people from a diversity of backgrounds. Chinese, Caucasian, African-American, Mexican, Asian.........And it was obvious that the ripple effects of this woman's life would go on and on and on. And as we prayed, we were one step closer to Heaven because of this hero who had lived amongst us.

Today be blessed!!

❧ *Land That Plane* ❧

"Teach us to number our days that we may grow in wisdom."

—Psalm 90:12 (GWT)

As I write this I'm sitting across the bay from the San Francisco Airport. I would have never thought that sitting across from an airport would be a serene locale but even amidst the roar of the jet engines a strange sense of peace has overcome me. Now you have to know that this is an unbelievably busy airport. In the time that I've been here I can't tell you how many planes I've seen take-off and land. There appear to be two main runways. The shorter runway services the standard jets that serve our Continental U.S. These planes speed up quick and disappear even quicker. The first plane veers off to the left and the one behind it veers off to the right. The next one may go straight into the horizon and the one after does a full u-turn and heads back in the direction it left. Then there are the International flights. These planes are like nothing I've ever seen. They make their way to a longer runway and if you saw them you would know why. They are HUGE!!! I've never seen a jet so large. I was told these are the newer Airbuses. Their engines seem to roar way before they move and as they start down the runway it seems impossible that they will ever get off the ground but somehow, through sheer determination, they manage to launch and suddenly there mass is eclipsed by their elegance as they maneuver the sky. They're off but no matter which way they go, they all have their course set and they all have a destination.

Suddenly my focus shifts and I'm drawn to the planes coming in. This is a spectacle in itself. As you scour this horizon, you suddenly realize that they're everywhere. These tiny dots are scattered throughout the sky awaiting their turn at the runway. From afar they seem to be moving at their target in slow motion. In fact it doesn't even seem like some of them are moving at all. But you know this can't be since these passenger jets fly at speeds of 250 miles an hour. From this viewpoint you couldn't tell. In an instant they're here and suddenly you know how much of an illusion it was. In fact you watch and hold your breath as they land, hoping the brakes don't fail as the terminal draws closer and closer. All of this activity happens so quickly and with such precision that I suddenly realize how grateful I am that a power greater than me is orchestrating this precision dance. Then it dawns on me......

These planes are a lot like our lives. We all come in so many different shapes and sizes and we all start down our runway heading in our own pre-determined direction. As we take flight, the controls are thrust into our hands and we begin to navigate the skies of our lives. Sometimes we fly low unsure of exactly where we are going. Sometimes we soar to heights we never thought we could have achieved. Sometimes there's so much turbulence we're sure we're going to break up and sometimes the storm is so bad we're sure we're lost. Unfortunately sometimes we even have to crash land even though there is someone greater than ourselves orchestrating our dance. Other times it even seems like we're not moving at all like those planes approaching the runway, but in reality life is flying by at hundreds of miles an hour. And this is where I really started to think. I know that this flight called life is passing by and it's up to me to enjoy the ride. Because one day, one day in the not too distant future, I will also be approaching my destination. In fact this is where we will differ from the planes; we will all reach our destination. We will all approach that moment when we will stand before the Creator of Heaven and Earth and we will be asked about our flight and what will we say. That it happened too quickly, that we missed the runway, that we didn't stop and enjoy the wonderful ride we had been so greatly blessed with. What will we say? I can't honestly answer that question yet since I haven't landed my plane. But there is one thing I hope…..that when I do arrive, that great Navigator will say, "Well done. You maneuvered the storms, handled the turbulence, and soared to unbelievable heights. Now it's time to retire, to relax and enjoy the destination." How wonderful it will be to hear those words……. (or some variation there of... ☺).

On that day, and today I will be blessed.

Today, be blessed with me.

One-Liners

"Words kill, words give life;

they're either poison or fruit—you choose."

-Proverbs 18:21 (MSG)

It was one of those days. It seemed as if things could not go my way no matter what I tried. I can't say it was a complete disaster of a morning. It just hadn't turned out the way I had planned and my spirit was defeated. I knew I needed to shake these feelings of frustration but for some reason, on this day, I couldn't. I also knew that if anything was going to change, the start of it all came with me and my attitude. But sometimes changing our attitude is easier said than done. I stepped out for an early lunch and a much needed break. And then it happened, a one-liner that went like this,

"You are an amazing man!"

Plain and simple, five little words that added up to a short sentence but its impact was beyond its length and its depth beyond its complexity. It came in the form of a text and it came from my amazing wife. These five little words stopped me in my tracks and changed my day. They brightened my mood and transformed my outlook on the tasks ahead. Suddenly I went from sullen to encouraged. The afternoon changed because my attitude changed. And it was all because of a simple one-liner.

How powerful our words are. How true Proverbs is. It is so easy to ruin another's day by speaking poison or even ruin a life by constantly using words that kill a spirit. On the other hand, a barrage of encouraging words uplift and can take others to new heights. And it's all in the power of the tongue. The funny thing, it doesn't take that much effort to make such huge impact. On this day, it only took my wife about five seconds to make five hours worth of impact. In fact, that's not even fair because the impact is being felt as I write this. Multiple deposits like these make for a lifetime of savings. And we all have the power.

Needless to say, I wrote her back and thanked her. She was uplifted. And today I uplift you,

"You are amazing!!!"

This is true! No matter what the circumstances; No matter what the day; No matter what the world tells you,

"You are amazing!!!"

I think so and God knows so. I am telling you and God tells you over and over in His Word.

"You are amazing!!"

So today be encouraged. Know that you are loved. And when you are uplifted, lift someone else up. It's our choice. As we are given life, let's give life. And together, we can all be blessed.

On the Wings of Eagles

"But those who hope in the LORD

will renew their strength.

They will soar on wings like eagles;

they will run and not grow weary,

they will walk and not be faint."

-Isaiah 40:3 (NIV)

Eagles are amazing creatures. They are very loyal taking one mate for life. They go places no other animal goes and see things from a different viewpoint. They are strong, agile hunters. But there is one characteristic that really inspires me. Eagles are very aware of there surroundings and can sense when there is a storm coming. However, unlike other creatures that see the storm approaching and head for cover, eagles will turn and fly to a spot that puts them directly in its center. Here they set their wings and wait. As the storm approaches, they will use the power of the storm to lift them higher and by the time it is at its peak they are soaring over it. What an analogy!!

I can look back at my life and see the times where I was that creature that ducked and ran for cover when life's storms approached. I can also look back and see how God would pull me out of my seclusion and take me through the storm. Now my prayer is to imitate that eagle and trust God as I fly into and over the storm!! The blessing of an eagle mentality....

What storm are you facing this week? Maybe it's a long week at work with goals that you're unsure of how you'll accomplish. Or something much more serious like health issues which show no sign of breaking soon. Maybe its financial, maybe it has to do with relationships.

Whatever it is, ask God to change your perspective. Look into the storm, set your wings, and soar over the top of it where you should be. Be an eagle!!

Lord,
Today we thank you for the day. We thank you for the assurance that you are with us in the day. We also praise You in the storm. Show us the truth of Your Word and renew our strength. Teach us to run and not grow weary. But most of all, give us that eagle mentality that we may soar above the clouds. This is Your promise and we lay hold of it in Jesus name.
Amen.

≈⁓ *Shine* ≈⁓

"Let me tell you why you are here. You're here to be salt-seasoning that

brings out the God-flavors of this earth. If you lose your saltiness, how will

people taste godliness? You've lost your usefulness and will end up in the

garbage.

"Here's another way to put it: You're here to be light, bringing out the

God-colors in the world. God is not a secret to be kept. We're going public

with this, as public as a city on a hill. If I make you light-bearers, you

don't think I'm going to hide you under a bucket, do you? I'm putting

you on a light stand. Now that I've put you there on a hilltop, on a light

stand—shine! Keep open house; be generous with your lives. By opening

up to others, you'll prompt people to open up with God, this generous

Father in heaven."

-Matthew 5:13-16 (MSG)

Can I be honest. There are times in my life that I get
tired. Tired of doing the "right" thing. Tired of going
the extra mile. Tired of giving. Tired of waking up
early and sending out these messages, wondering if

they're making a difference. But then I get reminded of why I'm here....

I participated in a walk for life to benefit a local church's food ministry. As soon as I got there I saw people I knew needing help. A mom of a friend walked up to me and asked me if I had seen her son. He hasn't returned her calls and she knows he's lost out in the world again. We agreed to join in prayer for him. I turned and saw another friend I had grown up with. We hadn't seen each other in years. We started talking and she was trying to get her life back together. She asked if I was still in church. I replied I was and encouraged her with the things God had helped me go through. She thanked me and left. Then the walk began.

As we were walking, we passed a park where the homeless people in our community hang out. I was stunned as I saw three more people I knew there. I made sure to greet each one. At this point I knew God had timed this walk. He had put me in a place to remind me of why I was here. He had allowed me to be reminded of all the hurting people that were so close around me. I also knew in that instant that none of these people planned to be where they were and that I could have just as easily been there. But the greatest reminder: that I had a message of hope for these people!!

The moral to this story.
We have purpose. Purpose beyond ourselves.
Purpose that carries with it destiny. Sometimes the flesh

can get tired but when the spirit is reminded of what's at stake, the honor of what we do and who we do it for arises and the fire is stirred. Bottom-line: people are counting on us. God is counting us. He prepared us. He takes us through things so we can honestly encourage the next person. In the words of my Pastor, He makes our mess our message, our test our testimony, our story His glory. These people are all around us; in your neighborhood, at your job, and, quite possibly in your home. Never stop going the extra mile!! Trust God for the results and one day in Heaven you'll have your treasure. Simply do as He says, Shine my friends, Shine.....

Lord,
You have seen something in us that too often we don't see in ourselves. You have given us the honor to be your chosen ambassadors to spread a message of hope. You have given us the ability to shine when we simply reflect you. Forgive us for the times we've hidden this lamp and help us to boldly stand on the hill and proclaim your goodness. Let our actions speak greater than our words and bless us with the greatest gift of all, let us make a difference in the lives we touch.
Always for your glory.
Amen.

❦ *Déjà vu* ❦

Suddenly my raced mind raced back to a time in the not too distant past. The nurse was providing easing small talk as the moment approached. Any conversation to ease the anxiety was welcome. The doors opened with the push of a button and my gurney was wheeled in. The atmosphere changed. Here was a team of individuals ready to do their assigned task. One got me off the gurney and over to the table. Another was telling me what was going to happen, which is always a haze. Another hooked up the oxygen tube to my nose and the IV to my arm. Yet another positioned me, sterilized my abdomen area, and marked the spot. Finally the doctor came in and with his last words said, I closed my eyes and it happened.

In the midst of all of this activity, in the midst of this crowd, up to this point, I had felt all alone. Everything going on around me was a whir of activity and I was the center of it but I was somehow detached as if it was surreal, not really happening. Quite honestly, anxiety was my only companion up to now. Once again, suddenly, the tables turned. I can't explain it and I don't think you can understand it unless you've experienced it. And if you've experienced it, you know exactly what I'm talking about. As my eyes closed I remembered God's personal words to me, *"I will never leave you nor forsake you...."* It happened....PEACE!! In the midst of that crowd it was just God and me. No one else mattered. Nothing else was important. It was only His presence and His promise, *"I'm here."* I smiled and off I went.....

Déjà vu. In this incident it was only a checkup; a biopsy to make sure everything was going as planned. In the last incident it had been a surgery that had saved my life. But in both, the moment was the same. I was there....and He was with me. And there was peace, the prize of faith. And I was blessed.

Today, be blessed with me. Don't wait for an anxiety ridden moment. Close your eyes, point your thoughts up, and smile. You are not alone. There is PEACE.

❦ *Distracted* ❦

"About three o'clock in the morning Jesus came toward them, walking on the

water. When the disciples saw him walking on the water, they were terrified. In

their fear, they cried out, "It's a ghost!" But Jesus spoke to them at once. "Don't

be afraid," he said. "Take courage. I am here!" Then Peter called to him, "Lord,

if it's really you, tell me to come to you, walking on the water."

"Yes, come," Jesus said.

So Peter went over the side of the boat and walked on the water toward Jesus.

But when he saw the strong wind and the waves, he was terrified and began to

sink. "Save me, Lord!" he shouted. Jesus immediately reached out and

grabbed him."

-Matthew 14:25-31 (NLT)

I recently learned a valuable lesson. I learned how
easily I can be distracted. My morning started out like
many others. I had a mini-conference to attend for
work and I had spent the night before reviewing
material for this event. I have a tendency to do this as I
don't like to be unprepared. When I awoke my folder I
had been reading was lying next to me and my mind
went back to the same place it had left off the night
before. I jumped up, ran through the morning "routine"

and headed out the door. About ten miles down the road it hit me, today was Friday! I had allowed myself to get so distracted by this task that I had forgotten the most important preparation of the day, I had forgotten about my time with God.

For over a year Friday mornings have been special times for me and God. I have woken up a little earlier than the norm, gotten out the laptop, and connected with the Lord through these morning writings. For me it is a wonderful time and it is my way of keeping my relationship with God fresh, alive, and on point. During these times God speaks to me, guides me, corrects me, and reassures me. And on this morning I had done like Peter, I had taken my eyes off of God and let the things of this world distract me.

It's funny because different things can distract and in this case it wasn't a bad thing. In fact being prepared and excelling at work is a good thing and it is something God wants us to do. I have done this for years and I know that any blessings I've received at my job have come from God. But I've also always strived to keep God in his proper place which is ahead of my job. And it was here that I felt suddenly convicted on my way to the mini-conference on this Friday morning.

You might say that it was only one Friday morning and it really isn't that big a deal, and in one sense you may be right. Missing only one Friday morning of these writings isn't the end of the world, and alone this one event does not mean I've walked away from God. It really wasn't the missing of this one event that hit me hard, it was the fact that I hadn't stopped to even say hello to the one who shares my home with me, the one I love, and the one who loves me and guides me through the day. I had simply walked out without even so much as a "Good Morning" to God. This to me was a big deal.

What would it be like if I did this to my wife? If even though her physical presence was there, I simply acted as if she wasn't. And what if I caught it that day but then it happened another.....and another. Where would our relationship end up? I shudder to even think about such a thing so I will awaken EVERY morning and tell her I love her, spend at least a few moments with her, and be blessed by her presence. Should it be any different with God even though His presence is spiritual and not physical? I have to say that for me it can't be. I need Him. I need His guidance. I need His counsel. I need HIM to truly be prepared for the day, no matter what task faces me. And that is why this small distraction was so big to me.

In the end I asked His forgiveness and of course He reached down, like He did for Peter, and lifted me back up. And I am breaking the "routine" and writing on Monday. Maybe it ended up being a good thing because things can become "routine" for us. So today I start afresh and also ask your forgiveness. I ask this because I have relationship with many of you and care about that relationship as well. And this is a way I stop and say, "Good Morning" to many of you. So a "Good Morning" it is. A blessed morning. I have started my day right. In fact, I have started my week right. And I pray that you too will start your week right, blessed with the Presence of the one who can make a difference in every aspect of our lives. I am reminded of a song by an artist named Toby Mac, "I don't want to gain the whole world, and lose my soul." There is nothing more important than our relationship with God. This is the one thing that will truly last an eternity. And that is the point to my story. Every day with God is a good day! Lord, help us not to forget that!!

Today be blessed.

❧ *Gray-Haired Wisdom* ❧

"Gray hair is a crown of glory;

it is gained by living a godly life."

-Proverbs 16:31 (NLT)

Life is filled with firsts. The first time you drive. Your first job. Your first date. Your first child. Your first…….. The list goes on and on. In fact, I've quoted the saying, "When is the last time you did something for the first time?" It's important that as we advance in age we don't get stuck in such routine that we never stretch ourselves to try new things, new ways, seek new adventures. Firsts are good, most of the time.

I recently had a "first" I wasn't expecting. My family and I had decided to go to the local movie theater. We hadn't been in a while and my eldest daughter was joining us so I was excited. Spending any time anywhere with the kids is great. As we walked up I stepped to the window to buy our tickets. The gentleman politely looked up, glanced at our group, and inquired, "One senior and two adults?" He caught me off guard….SENIOR????? Who was he talking about? I looked back and I didn't see anyone close except for my wife and she looks the same way she did when we married. Except at this time she's fighting back the giggles that are ready to burst out….SENIOR. I looked back and politely corrected the gentleman, "Uh, no Sir, three adults please." I get the tickets and turn around and by now my whole family is cracking up!! Me on the other hand, I'm still a little troubled. Am I really getting there? Am I really looking like a "SENIOR?" Well, as you can see it did get to me a bit. So much so that it almost felt like the gentleman made a derogatory comment. Of course I played it off as a good joke, my first time being asked if I qualified for the senior discount. Wow….

Once that initial shock wore off I started thinking about the comment and I realized, "Wow, I am "maturing." You know what? I'm glad. I started thinking about all the "bonehead" decisions I had made as a young man and all the things I had learned through the years. I suddenly realized I had been paid a compliment. My gray hairs are not signs of weakness but of age, wisdom, and maturity. I am blessed. Senior is not a bad word. In fact it means that the good Lord has blessed me with these wonderful years of life and with the wisdom that comes only by experience. It means I have "survived" the days of my youth and that the years to come are truly golden. I started looking into God's Word and I realized how lucky I was.

"You shall stand up before the gray head and honor the face of an old

man, and you shall fear your God: I am the LORD."

-Leviticus 19:32 (ESV)

"The glory of young men is their strength, gray hair the splendor of the

old."

-Proverbs 20:29 (NIV)

"Even in old age they will still produce fruit;

they will remain vital and green.

They will declare, "The LORD is just!

He is my rock!

There is no evil in him!"

-Psalm 92:14-15 (NLT)

"When I was a child, I spoke and thought and reasoned as a child. But when I

grew up, I put away childish things."

-1 Corinthians 13:11 (NLT)

I have matured and I have aged. In the midst of
passing time, I have grown. My years have brought me
clarity of thought and clearness of vision. I see as a
man and I am thankful to my God. By no means have I
"arrived" at the pinnacle of my development. I've still
got a lot to learn. But I've learned a lot too. I am
where I am and I will be blessed to be here!

If you are approaching or have reached these "golden"
years, congratulations!! If you are in your youth,
enjoy!! Wherever you are, be thankful!! Today is a new
day and it will pass quickly. Build good memories and

be fruitful in the moment. Rejoice. You are where you are meant to be. Gray haired or not.

Be blessed!!

❦ It's All in a Day ❦

"This is the day the LORD has made. We will rejoice and be glad in it."

-Psalm 118:24 (NLT)

What a difference a day makes.

I can't help but sit back and evaluate life and begin to tie together the events that have produced my 46 years of existence. I marvel at the fact that we can rise up in the morning hours and life can be completely different by that evening. I remember the day I got the news that my wife was pregnant and that soon life would be renewed through us. An amazing shift in the universe led to the blessing that I have today. Then the day that the child was born, words cannot describe the impact of that moment. I've been blessed with four days like that and on each of those days my life changed. Then there are those other days where the morning starts like any other and by that evening a gap is left in our heart by the memory of a loved one who is no longer here. A beloved aunt, a wonderful grandmother, a child, my mom……….

Those days we could all do without.

But they are a part of this stringed together sequence we call life. And the only way we will truly "be glad" in life is if we hold onto the one constant we have, God. In one given week my family gathered and we enjoyed a wonderful time together like we do every

Sunday. A few days later my family joined together in prayer over a close friend who had been shot. In the midst of the week a friend came to me and announced that she would soon be experiencing the miracle of life as she had just found out she was expecting a child. On that same day another friend struggled with an illness that was out of her control. I could go on and on of the mixture of times but in the end they are our days. They are our lives. They are the gift that God has given us and in each of them we can find moments to cry and moments to rejoice, reasons to be happy and sad. In the end, it is the day that God has made and because of Him we will rejoice because He has allowed us to experience it.

This particular week turned out okay. My friend who got shot is going to be okay. My friend who is going to have a child is going to be blessed. And my friend who is struggling with her illness will recover. And it all happens in a day......

Let this be your day and let it be blessed!

Perfect Love

"God is love....

No one has seen God, ever. But if we love one another, God dwells deeply

within us, and his love becomes complete in us, perfect love!"

- 1 John 4:8, 12 (MSG)

I know that the Bible says that no one has seen God but yesterday I saw Him. I saw Him in an 18 year old father. I saw a young man holding his 15 day old son with a care that went beyond words. It wasn't just the emotion I'm speaking of. It was his attentiveness to the child. I saw love.

This young man and his girlfriend were signing up for college. One was going days and the other evenings so they could take turns watching the baby. They wanted a better future for their child. As each one was called to a different counselor, the father graciously took the sleeping child. During the appointment, Dad kept one eye always on his infant. When the child awoke, he politely said excuse me and proceeded to take the child gently into his arms and comfort him, feed him, change him..... Whatever the child needed, the father provided. I saw God!!

The love I saw was the love God has for his children, for me. And I must confess it brought a tear to my eye. How God, in the midst of overseeing the universe, ALWAYS has an eye on me. How He is there meeting all my needs, holding me, comforting me, loving me, always wanting a better future for me. God was in front of me in the image of this young man. After all, this young man was made in the image of God.

Then another thought, God had this love for His own

Son Jesus. The Apostle John said, *"The Father loves the Son extravagantly."* This deeply rooted emotion that leads to action was birthed in Jesus. The amazing thing, it was transferred to us. What God did next is almost beyond comprehension. He gave this Son that He loved so much for us, for me!

"This is how God showed his love for us: God sent his only Son into the world so we might live through him. This is the kind of love we are talking about, not that we once upon a time loved God, but that he loved us and sent his Son as a sacrifice to clear away our sins and the damage they've done to our relationship with God."

- 1 John 4:9-10 (MSG)

Hence the tear. My friends, this is the Gospel, the Good News, the Love. The story tells itself. This is true and perfect love. This is God!!

Be blessed by the love of your Father!!

❧ *Just Care* ❧

"Teacher, which command in God's Law is the most important?"

Jesus said, "'Love the Lord your God with all your passion and prayer and intelligence.' This is the most important, the first on any list. But there is a second to set alongside it: 'Love others as well as you love yourself.' These two commands are pegs; everything in God's Law and the Prophets hangs from them."

-Matthew 22: 36b-40 (MSG)

I was recently asked what my goals for the year were and since I hadn't made any New Year's resolutions this year I hesitated. I explained in a broad kind of way that I was still in a mode of reflection and couldn't concretely answer. But this question did make me think because I have learned that no goals usually equates to no accomplishments. We have to have something to strive for.

So the weekend quest began. What are my goals for the year? What are the things I would like to see come to pass? What changes in myself would I like to strive for? Personally, professionally, spiritually, each area had to be examined. As I thought this through, my previous writings came to mind. I had set one goal already, to tackle these issues of required change as they appeared. With that in mind I was struggling to come up with a "list" of goals. But still…….

Then it hit me. Some of what I had accomplished last year had been done through pursuing a mark, but **everything** that I had attained definitely came from pursuing an attitude. In this instant it was as if God himself zapped me with a "Word of Knowledge," just care!

Just care. Two small words with such huge impact that I could stop and ponder on them for days to come, but two words which were also so simple that they didn't take much thought or explanation, just care. Imagine that. If everything I did, everything I involved myself in revolved around these two words, my life would be dramatically changed. If I cared more about my relationship with my family, it would rise to new heights! If I cared more about my role in God's Kingdom, the accomplishments would be milestones! If I cared more about my performance at the place God has allowed me to be employed, all would see the difference!! And this is not to say that I don't care now. It is simply meant to remind that we can always care a bit more and this bit more can make a huge difference. Suddenly these two words transformed in my mind to one: passion. Lord, allow me to live a life of passion. Let me live with such an intense overpowering emotion that it encompasses my entire life. Let me remember that this word, passion, is connected to you and the sufferings up to the cross. Let me see this as an example of love. In the end let this passion translate to people and let me do one thing, just care.

So there it is, my number one priority for the year and every year to come. It's out in existence now and all of you can help me to be accountable to this goal. With that said I leave you with a thought. Will you join me

on this quest and do one thing, just care. Our world will
be different and we will make that difference.

Today, may you be blessed with this thought!

Just Care....

❦ *May I Serve You?* ❦

"But among you it will be different. Whoever wants to be a leader among you

must be your servant, and whoever wants to be first among you must become your

slave. For even the Son of Man came not to be served but to serve others and to give

his life as a ransom for many."

-Matthew 20:26-29 (NLT)

What a concept! Here we are nearing the end of this leader's "rule" in His current position and He wants to ensure that all have clearly gotten the message. Some of His followers have been arguing about their place in the "organization" so much so that they have come to Him and asked if they can have the number two and three spots in the chain of command. Jesus must have looked at them and thought, "You still don't get it..." Here I wonder, has He looked at me and thought the same thing......

You know I'm sure His attitude is much different than mine and when He sees I don't get it He doesn't get tired of teaching the same lesson or frustrated like I might. Instead He puts examples in front of me and reminds me of the lessons He taught. He reminds how as He is about to share His last meal with His "team" here on Earth, He kneels before them, removes their sandals, and begins to wash their feet. He reminds me how the focus was to be outward, how life wasn't to be all about me, me, me, but about others. He reminds me of the great joys of service and the rewards which are

96

not physical but worth more than all the gold in the world.

Then He takes it a step further. He reminds me that sometimes this service will be costly. It will not be comfortable. It will be performed to some that may not see nor appreciate the sacrifice. But it is the way of life in His Kingdom all the same. He shows that we must be so convinced of this philosophy that we lay all down, even our lives for the sake of others. And then, like He does, He senses how difficult this can be so He comforts me with words that I can understand,

"If you try to hang on to your life, you will lose it. But if you give up your life for

my sake, you will save it."

-Matthew 16:25 (NLT)

I'm not losing anything by giving up the focus on me. I'm gaining everything. It is here that I find my worth, my purpose. It is here that I gain the strength for the day. And it is here that I find true joy and peace. I get it, for the moment. I'm sure I'll need another reminder. I'm sure I'll get a little off course. But the "Good News", He'll be there to lead me back in the right direction. And in this life I will continue to be blessed.

Today, be blessed with me.

"Don't worry about anything; instead, pray about everything. Tell God

what you need, and thank him for all he has done. Then you will

experience God's peace, which exceeds anything we can understand. His

peace will guard your hearts and minds as you live in Christ Jesus."

-Philippians 4:6-7 (NLT)

Don't worry.....
Easier said than done, would you agree? Doesn't it
sometimes seem to be a part of our very human .
nature to look at the unknown and immediately
become anxious. For some reason I was prompted to
look up that word anxious and here's what I found:

-characterized by extreme uneasiness of mind or
brooding fear about an event (as an emergency) that
may, but is not certain to, occur : worried.

This really made me think. How many times had I
been so worried about something that never came to
be? Some of the things that come to mind: worried
about the results of Dr.'s tests; worried about
money; worried about my kids; worried about my
job; simply worried about life!

But I've learned a couple of things in this lifetime of
worry. First, I'm gonna worry. Don't get me wrong.
I'm not saying that I've given in to this "woe is me"
life of gloom and doom like the guy from Gulliver's
Travels (you old timers will remember the cartoon).
Sometimes there are very real situations in our lives
that evoke this feeling. No matter how hard we try to
control it, it just spills out. I've come to believe that's
natural. But I've also come to know that we don't
have to live in the natural!

There's another word that comes into play here and I've learned that it can overcome the natural: Faith. I looked it up and here's what I found:

-firm belief in something for which there is no proof : complete trust

It also talks about the unknown but in a different perspective-complete trust. And who should this trust be in? Doctors? Our jobs? Our money? No. It needs to be in God. You have to know God. You have to know that whether or not that thing you're worrying about ever comes to pass, He will always be with you. And how do you get this complete trust, this faith? Honestly, by simply going through things and coming out okay. I can write this because I've been through a few things and they've turned into blessings to encourage others.

So the next time you're faced with those moments of despair, don't beat yourself up because you have them. Just simply don't stay in them. Let the stronger of the two words defeat the other. Remember, no matter how you feel, He is faithful. Be encouraged!

Lord,
Thank you for this day. You have blessed us with it and we will rejoice in it. Help us to do so regardless of our circumstances. Give us the supernatural that we may overcome the natural. Build our faith through these moments that we may develop a complete trust in you. We are eternally grateful. Thank you! Amen.

꩜ *A Glimpse of Heaven* ꩜

"I saw—it took my breath away!—the Lamb standing on Mount Zion, 144,000

standing there with him, his Name and the Name of his Father inscribed on their

foreheads. And I heard a voice out of Heaven, the sound like a cataract, like the crash

of thunder.

And then I heard music, harp music and the harpists singing a new song

before the Throne...."

-Revelation 14:1 (MSG)

I'm sure we've all wondered what Heaven is going to be like. There's the classic walking through the clouds seeing angels strumming harps. There's the thought of reunion with loved ones gone before us. There's the thought of the mansion Jesus said He went to prepare for us which sits on the streets of gold. Or the supper table where we will feast with the King. But recently I believe the Lord blessed my wife and I with one of the most amazing glimpses into Heaven and it was the place of praise, the worship service that will be the center point of our existence.

It happened on a Saturday evening. A group of well-known Christian artists got together and went on a "Rock and Road Worship Tour" where there whole incentive was not to make money but to worship our Lord with as many others who would join as possible. I know this because the event was held at the "Arena formerly known as Arco" and the tickets were only $10. This event featured famous artists including Mercy Me, Jars of Clay, and LeCrae just to name a few. The event was so successful that the venue quickly filled to capacity and they had to turn people away. I looked it up and that is 17,300 people joined together to worship. 17,300 people from different churches and different walks of life. It was amazing. As each group came on the energy just kept intensifying and every one was of one mind and one accord. Each artist(s) had their own style but each one had the same purpose. Whether you like contemporary pop, hard rock, rap or worship, all was represented. But then it happened...the glimpse....

Towards the end of the concert one of the groups, Mercy Me, came on and they did an offering for a worthwhile cause. No arms twisted, simply a request to help. As the gentleman was speaking you could hear his heart of appreciation and during this time there suddenly came a silence that I wouldn't have thought possible for a place filled with 17,300 people. And then a song, Heart of Worship, began:

"When the music fades
All is stripped away
And I simply come
Longing just to bring
Something that's of worth
That will bless your heart

I'll bring You more than a song
For a song in itself
Is not what You have required
You search much deeper within
Through the way things appear

You're looking into my heart

I'm coming back to the heart of worship
And it's all about You
It's all about You, Jesus
I'm sorry, Lord, for the thing I've made it
When it's all about You
It's all about You, Jesus"

As we listened, we joined in with this song as it seemed like everyone knew it. Suddenly something had me to stop singing and just listen and I heard it! The entire arena had become one voice and this voice was the most beautiful sound you could imagine. It was as if every vocal chord was suddenly blessed with the perfect harmony, pitch, note, that existed and all were in perfect sync. I knew in that instant the angelic choir of heaven had joined us. I looked at my wife and she was hearing the same exact thing. And immediately we both broke into tears. God had allowed us a glimpse into Heaven.

Friends, worship is an amazing thing. If you've never experienced this get yourselves to a place where lovers of Christ are gathered and get your own glimpse. Experience the miracle. You will never be the same.

Be blessed!!

(Heart of Worship by Michael W. Smith)

"Be good to me, God—and now! I've run to you for dear life.

I'm hiding out under your wings

until the hurricane blows over.

I call out to High God,

the God who holds me together.

He sends orders from heaven and saves me,

he humiliates those who kick me around.

God delivers generous love,

he makes good on his word."

-Psalm 57:1-3 (MSG)

God gave me a clear reminder of what Church was all about.

As I arrived I noticed a young lady with who appeared to be with her grandmother. I introduced myself and immediately this wonderful woman started to take me on a journey. She explained that she was there supporting her granddaughter because when she was 15 years old someone had taken her to a church and supported her. She was 81 now but she spoke with such clarity and passion that it was as if it had just happened yesterday. It was a wonderful moment the day she met Jesus. She then spoke of her father who

103

after that time went on to become a minister. She told of her husband who was the epitome of a good man in her eyes and I could sense the deep love that they had shared. He had gone to be with the Lord but she never questioned why. She simply gave thanks for having had time with such a wonderful man. She came to a point where she spoke of her children and how recently she had lost her younger daughter. A tear swelled up but still she trusted in God. In a matter of 15 minutes I felt as if I had shared a piece of this saintly guest's experiences and life. I knew that because of these few minutes my life was enriched. I watched her as she walked in to the service knowing she was walking in to a familiar place even if the building was different than she was accustomed to. After all, it wasn't the building she was after but the One who building was dedicated to.

The next thing I knew there was a great shift and on the platform there must have been at least 10 couples holding their baby's ready for a dedication service. Now here was the beginning of life, the innocence of youth, and the mystery of a time yet to be lived. As I recalled the conversation above, I prayed that each of these children would be blessed with the richness of life I had heard of before. Here was a journey beginning, and a journey that would require the love and dedication of not only the parents but of all those gathered. After all, it really does take a village....

Following this a young woman and her father would come up. She simply shared a heart of gratitude. This young lady had been in a terrible accident but God had brought her through and she just wanted everyone to know that she was thankful for the support. Then her father spoke and his words were truly inspiring. In the midst of this tragedy he still spoke of God's goodness and presence. His message was simple but powerful, when God asks, "What can I do for you?" don't be too proud or self sufficient to ignore the question. When God asks it's because He's ready to deliver. You could tell that for this family, that is exactly what He had done, delivered.

With so much said already, the Pastor took only a few moments but gave a powerful illustration of our part in the upbringing of our youth. It was very simple but delivered the message. He brought a bent branch with extra twigs hanging off and showed how this branch, with the proper molding, could become a straight arrow ready to hit any bulls eye. It was a perfect analogy to what I thought was the end of service.

As my wife and I were greeting people on their way out another woman approached us. We stepped into our welcome center and before we knew it we were immersed in prayer for a mom who had been diagnosed with terminal cancer. Talking to her you wouldn't have known it. You wouldn't have guessed she had already outlived the doctor's words because there was such radiance in her smile. Speaking to her I knew that this power could have only come from God himself. We gathered in a circle and trusted God even in this situation. She left thankful and encouraged. We left in awe of who God is and what He can do, deliver. In any circumstance or situation, He can deliver.

On any given Sunday......
For that matter, on any given day. God is waiting
with the simple question, "What can I do for you?" On
this day we had seen the question asked and the
request granted. Today He is asking you. Can you here
Him? Ask. He's there. "What can I do for you?"

Today be blessed and take Him up on His offer.

Conversion

"So we have stopped evaluating others from a human point of view. At one time we thought of Christ merely from a human point of view. How differently we know him now! This means that anyone who belongs to Christ has become a new person. The old life is gone; a new life has begun!"

-2 Corinthians 5:16-17 (NLT)

Recently at work we are going through a conversion of systems. This conversion is taking all of the information from one system and "converting" it into a new, improved system which is going to allow us to do so much more and do it more efficiently. Prior to the start of this project there was a lot of preparation and advance training getting us ready for this change. There was a lot of discussion on the benefits of this change. There was a sense of excitement and anticipation in the air for the coming of this change. Then the change happened.

In the first days that excitement filled the air and everyone was looking forward to this new way of doing things and we all jumped in head first. Then some reality started to set in on how much effort was needed when change occurs. The way we used to do things was gone and suddenly we had to look at everything different, or so we thought. Some of the daily tasks which were ingrained in us had to be approached differently and I have to admit that at times the old way was missed. It was missed even though it was such a cumbersome way of doing things. It was missed even though it required so much more to get to the same goal. Why? Because it was familiar. It's funny how sometimes new ways of doing things are avoided even though they're so much better simply because the comfort of where we are outweighs the discomfort of change.

God started speaking to me, like He does, and He reminded me of another time in my life when change was in the air. It was during a time when I first started to learn about God and His way of doing things. At first I started to hear of this new "system" and how much better it was. I started to imagine what life could be like in this "new world" and I got excited but I also hesitated. I hesitated because I was so ingrained in my old world. Even though this world brought with it so much pain and discomfort, I knew it. And knowing it brought a sense of familiarity which hindered the thought of change. What if I couldn't make it in this new world? What if the change was good but I wasn't ready for it? What if I failed and ended up right back where I started? All of this rose up in me but suddenly before I knew it I was in the midst of this new course of life and I couldn't turn back. The old way was there but I knew that this was my chance. This was my opportunity to improve and take on life the way it was meant to live. And while there were many moments of uneasiness and anxiety, I pressed on and today I am so blessed because I did. The "old system" could never compare to this new one. In fact, the only regret is that

I didn't do it sooner. But at the end of the day, the change occurred when it was supposed to.

So here we are at work and we're facing the challenge of this change. We realize that the old has gone and the new is here to stay. We've had our moments of uneasiness and anxiety, but something else has happened as well. We've had our victories. We've had those breakthrough moments when the realization hits that this new way is better. And with each coming victory, a new comfort arises in the new way. Old things pass and new things replace them. This is the lesson. Too often God takes me to this point in my life. This threshold where He is prompting me to change my ways in some area of my life and I hesitate because I am comfortable where I am, regardless of the amount of discomfort. But He builds the value of the change and thankfully for me, He brings the change and I am left with no choice but to embrace it. Actually, I guess I do have a choice and can keep running from it but the pain of staying the same way will eventually become greater than the pain of change so I've learned that the quicker I give in, the better the outcome. Out with the old and in with the new.

Today I pray that if God is speaking to you about something in your life that you embrace it. I pray that you take that plunge and jump into the newness He has for you. Whatever "it" is, God knows what He's doing and His change will only bring joy. Trust Him and bear the pain of change for the blessing of change will outweigh it so quickly that you'll look back and realize how good God really is.

☙ *Awakening* ☙

"After dark one evening, he came to speak with Jesus. "Rabbi," he said,

"we all know that God has sent you to teach us. Your miraculous signs are

evidence that God is with you."

Jesus replied, "I tell you the truth, unless you are born again, you cannot

see the Kingdom of God."

"What do you mean?" exclaimed Nicodemus. "How can an old man go

back into his mother's womb and be born again?"

-John 3:2-4 (NLT)

Bad things do happen to good people but God is still faithful. How can I say this? How can God take those bad things and bring good out of them?

My family lost a very wonderful woman who had done so much for many of us. It was devastating at the time and the memory still carries strong emotions. But out of those ashes something beautiful happened. A group of us pulled together in a difficult situation and have now become closer than ever. However, even greater, a miracle happened.

It didn't happen overnight. In fact, like many miracles, it is still unfolding. But what has unfolded out of those ashes has blossomed into a beautiful expression of God's ability to bring good out of bad and His faithfulness through every situation. I've seen my Aunt's Daughter and Granddaughter born again!!

In both of them I see a glow and a love for the Lord that is beyond words. I see the restoration of a relationship between a Heavenly Father and His earthly children. I see love and I see God and I am blessed! I also know that my Aunt would be very proud.

I know that we all wished things to be different and I don't believe that God wished this on my Aunt for an end result. He simply brought good out of bad. That's who He is and that's what He does.

Now every year on her birthday, we stop and give thanks for all she did. And we ask God for a favor, to deliver our message, "We love and will see you soon!!"

Lord,
Help us when bad things happen never to blame you but instead to lean on you and look for your loving kindness. Let us remember that all things work together for the good, if we continue to love you. Thank you for the times we have together with our families, especially the times we had with our departed loved ones. And, most importantly, thank you for being with us through every situation. We love you...

Be blessed!

"Don't be impressed with your own wisdom.

Instead, fear the Lord and turn away from evil.

Then you will have healing for your body and strength for your

bones....

.....My child, don't reject the Lord's discipline,

and don't be upset when he corrects you.

For the Lord corrects those he loves,

just as a father corrects a child in whom he delights."

-Proverbs 3:6-8, 11-12 (MSG)

It came out of nowhere. I was in a conversation and something came out that wasn't right. I don't even think the person I was talking to caught it but I knew my heart and God knew my heart and I winced. In an instant I felt the fear.

I'm not sure if you can understand this but I truly pray you can. It wasn't a fear because of the person in front of me. It was a fear that in that instant I had displeased God and in an instant I felt His conviction. This happens and when it does I don't like it. Why? Quite frankly it makes me uncomfortable. Second, Gods done too much for me to make Him displeased.

God reminded me of this as one of the men

taught on the fear of the Lord at church. He brought out that this type of fear was needed in our lives in order to truly be blessed. Sometimes I think we can forget just who God is. We like the loving, grace-giving, encouraging, lift-me-up God but would rather not deal with the "that-makes-me-uncomfortable" God. But would God be God if He didn't do this? Would I be a father if I never corrected my son? Would this be love? Of course not. I've got to take the discipline with the encouragement. Besides, this is the evidence that He loves me as His Word says.

Thank God for that!! Even though my flesh doesn't like these moments, my Spirit says thank you. What do I fear more? Not getting these feelings of conviction. It is these feelings that keep me, or return me, to the proper course.

So the next time God makes you uncomfortable about something in your life, don't run away from it or ignore Him. After all, it's only Dad trying to bless His child. As the saying goes, Father knows best!

Lord, thank you for the feelings of uneasiness. For those times when our stomachs turn and our muscles tighten because of your convictions. Help us to never forget that you are God and to live our lives with a fear that respects this fact. We thank you for your discipline because this demonstrates true love. Never let us lose this for if we do, we've lost you. And then we've lost all.....
In your blessed name we pray.
Amen.

Be blessed!!

In the Good Times

"It happened that as he made his way toward Jerusalem, he crossed over the

border between Samaria and Galilee. As he entered a village, ten men, all

lepers, met him. They kept their distance but raised their voices, calling out,

"Jesus, Master, have mercy on us!"

Taking a good look at them, he said, "Go, show yourselves to the priests."

They went, and while still on their way, became clean. One of them, when he

realized that he was healed, turned around and came back, shouting his

gratitude, glorifying God. He kneeled at Jesus' feet, so grateful. He couldn't

thank him enough—and he was a Samaritan.

Jesus said, "Were not ten healed? Where are the nine? Can none be found to

come back and give glory to God except this outsider?" Then he said to him,

"Get up. On your way. Your faith has healed and saved you."

-Luke 17:11-19 (MSG)

This past weekend I truly realized how far my
relationship with God had come. It was my Father's
birthday and we decided to have the party at a local
park. What usually happens with events like this is that
things start to go wrong. But Sunday was different. We
had a wonderful service at church and headed home to

get ready. When we got there everything was in place. I loaded the truck and off we went. When we got to the lake, there was a perfect spot right next to the water waiting for us. As I began to BBQ, the coals were just right and the meat came out perfect (this was really strange for me because I'm known for my jerky...lol).

As our loved ones started arriving, I realized that everyone we invited showed up. There were just enough people to make it intimate but not too many to make it out of hand. As we finished eating, there was just enough food. No one was left hungry and there weren't so many leftovers that they went to waste. My son and I set up the volleyball net and it actually stood on the first try. I looked over at my dad and he was smiling, happy, and content on this day that was meant to honor him. It was truly a perfect day.

What does this have to do with my relationship with God? Well, it happened on the way home. We stood until sunset and finally loaded everything up. Everyone had gone their way and I was driving home alone contemplating the day. As the music was playing, an overwhelming spirit of gratitude came over me. Suddenly I realized how much of a blessing I had just received. God had just blessed me with this wonderful time with my family and the miracle was that I realized that the day had come from Him. I stopped and began to praise Him. This is the change.

There was a time in my life when the only time I acknowledged God was when something bad happened or when I needed something. Then I was sure to be found calling out to Him. Now I know that even in those times, God heard my pleas and was there every time. Whether He changed the circumstances or simply got me through them, He was always willing to respond.

But this past weekend I realized how good it is to spend time with God in the good moments of life as well as the bad. I enjoyed a blessed day with my father on earth and my Father in Heaven. I didn't have to wait to seek God in disaster, I saw him in blessing and I was blessed. And, like the leper in Luke's story, I went back and I praised Him. God has truly changed my relationship with Him. Now I know that He is the God of the good as well as the Savior of the bad. He is God and He is good!!

.

Today, whatever your circumstance, stop and praise Him. If times are good, thank Him for them. If they're not so good, thank Him for His promise of never leaving or forsaking you. Either way, be like the one who returned not like the nine who forgot. The blessing of God is that He is always glad to hear from His children so..........Father's day or not.......say Hi to Dad (Our Father Who Art In Heaven) today!!!

Father, you are so good to us. If we call out to you in desperate times you don't hold it against us. You cherish our cries and reach down to help. Help us to remember you not only in those times but also in the times of blessing. The times when everything is going right and we have need of nothing. Help us to stop and not only pray for needs but praise for your presence. Help us to realize we have truly been healed. You are our Father and we are your children. Thank you for this wonderful relationship and today we will stop and simply be thankful because you are God and you are good!!

In your name we pray.

Amen.

116

"For everything there is a season,

a time for every activity under heaven.

A time to be born and a time to die.

A time to plant and a time to harvest.

A time to kill and a time to heal.

A time to tear down and a time to build up.

A time to cry and a time to laugh.

A time to grieve and a time to dance.

A time to scatter stones and a time to gather stones.

A time to embrace and a time to turn away.

A time to search and a time to quit searching.

A time to keep and a time to throw away.

A time to tear and a time to mend.

A time to be quiet and a time to speak.

A time to love and a time to hate.

A time for war and a time for peace."

~Ecclesiastes 3 (NLT)

Have you ever faced one of those days where you wake up and you realize that once it's over your life will never be the same?

As I look back on my life, I see decisions made and

courses taken and I've learned that each had value. Whether good or bad, each taught me something. Each one helped mold and develop me. And I don't regret any one.

But then there are the decisions made that were so right that you know they were a part of God-ordained destiny. That is how I am feeling today. Years ago God looked down and saw the desires of my heart. I had always wanted to pursue an education but had thought that chapter in my life had passed. Well since all things are possible with God I was quickened to take a step of faith and returned to college. Here something began to happen. I began to gain an extended family. When it came time to graduate I was blessed to be offered a position with this same college and the family continued to grow. Through the years many family members have come and gone but each one still holds a special place in my heart. Today I am the family member that is moving away. You see, today will be my last day at a college campus that has been a part of my life for over 10 years!

What does it all boil down to: People! While, just like family members who move away, I know the relationships will not end. I also know that I will miss the day to day interactions with people I've grown to love and respect so much. I am a better man because of them.

My point in this reflection? Appreciate those around you!! Whether it is a son, a spouse, or a co-worker, each one was placed there by God for a purpose and each one has influenced your life.

While today I know that one chapter in my life will close and another one open, I know that this chapter was perfectly written.

Today I am a blessed man!!!
Be blessed with me!!!

"A deep sense of awe came over them all, and the apostles performed many miraculous signs and wonders. And all the believers met together in one place and shared everything they had. They sold their property and possessions and shared the money with those in need. They worshiped together at the Temple each day, met in homes for the Lord's Supper, and shared their meals with great joy and generosity— all the while praising God and enjoying the goodwill of all the people. And each day the Lord added to their fellowship those who were being saved."

-Acts 2:43-47 (NLT)

Recently I had to face a situation that none of us would wish on even our worst enemy, an old friend lost his first born daughter. This is the second time in a year I've witnessed this. Months ago another friend lost his baby girl. I can only say witnessed because I cannot sit here and pretend to know the depth of their pain and loss. I can only have compassion, a deep sense of hurt for them, and a hope that in the midst of this that God is present. But if I've learned anything in these situations, it's that I can't explain God. When facing someone with something as deep as this, I can simply stand by their side and share a tear. I can hope for them and I can pray for them.

As my wife and I made contact with this couple one thing became obvious, friends and family poured out in support of this injured group. Not only did they share in their grief but they shared in their burdens. A local church opened its doors and a benefit luncheon was held to raise finances and it was very successful. People came out in droves and shared what they had. At the service multitudes came out and their mere presence showed that this young life had touched so many in the years here that there was no way it was lived in vain. A thank you statement was given by the family for all of the food, flowers, money, etc. that they had been blessed with. During this time of tragedy, the "goodwill of all the people" manifested itself and this family was touched. And I believe that in this goodwill, God was present.

Like I said, I cannot dare to try to stand in God's place and begin to try and explain why things like this happen. But I can say that it is good to see people come together and share in the burdens this life places on all of us, great and small. And I can pray that this spirit of supporting and helping those around us would not only materialize in times of great need, but in times of small need as well. While this was truly a blessing to see the help this family received in their time of need, their time of need has just begun and they will need these caring hearts around them for months/years to come. But thank God there is hope, hope in Him and hope in the Spirit He gives us to continue these acts of kindness. After all, isn't that what He's constantly doing for us, acts of kindness.

Lord,

help us to reflect you by focusing on the needs of those around us more than our own. The world will truly be a better place.

Amen (Let it be)!!

Gotta Have It

"As the deer longs for streams of water,

so I long for you, O God.

I thirst for God, the living God.

When can I go and stand before him?"

-Psalm 42:1-2 (NLT)

Any Cold Stone fans out there? In my city the creamery sits next to the movie theater and any time we go downtown the one accompanies the other. I struggle with this place because of my diabetes. Even though it is under control (thank God), I really have two choices. Do I stick with the "Sinless San Fat" non-fat no sugar added ice cream and go with the "Gotta Have It" size or do I cheat and indulge myself with another choice but lower my desire down to the "Like It" category.

Both have issues. Let's just say the sinless choice kind of upsets me. First it has this name referring to living without sin which refers to a religious way of living and it tastes blah!! Not only does it upset me because it tastes blah but because somehow in my mind this is the idea that I had about living a life for God before I knew Him. I thought it was going to be blah. I thought to myself, how terrible tasting and boring a life like that must be. I would rather cheat and live the "Gotta Have

It" life. Little did I know that this was the furthest thing from the truth.

Now the issue with the cheating and having the "Like It" category, I don't just like it, I gotta have it!!! Or so my mind thinks. The reality is I don't. It's just what I've conditioned myself into thinking. Really, I have a choice to make and two things to categorize. Is staying healthy and living longer in the "Like It," "Love It," or "Gotta Have It" category and where does that leave my desire for this treat. I want to tell myself I gotta have both but the reality is one pushes the other to the bottom. Issue number two, I hate these choices!!

Isn't that how life is? Especially spiritual life…..
I'm in a great situation because God has shown me that a life with Him is the best tasting, most desirable "treat" I could ever experience. Nothing can even come close to comparing. I know this but sometimes I'm afraid I put this reality back into the "Like It" category. How? By filling my life with so many other things that I "Gotta Have" that little time is left for cultivating this relationship with the greatest "Gotta Have It" in the universe, God. Instead I say I "Gotta Have It" but live like I just "Like It." Not good….

So today my prayer is simple but needs great power to make it come to pass. Today I pray that God himself would help me to change the desires of my heart. That my categories (priorities) would be properly aligned. That the lines of the "Like Its," Love Its," and Gotta Have Its" would be clearly drawn and then that my vision would stay clear. Truth is I'm sure the lines will get blurred at times, but if I keep drawing closer to the source of the greatest joy in my life, I will always be reminded of Cold Stone and God will always be in the "Gotta Have It" section of my life. The sweet desires of life are tempting but not worth cutting out the things I need for true joy and happiness.

Ouch!! Sorry "Peanut Butter Cup Perfection" but you've just been dropped in ranking. There are more important things that I "Gotta Have."

Lord, help us all with our "Like Its," "Love Its," and "Gotta Have Its" so we can truly be blessed!!

Valley of Dry Bones

"God grabbed me. God's Spirit took me up and set me down in the middle of an open plain strewn with bones. He led me around and among them—a lot of bones! There were bones all over the plain—dry bones, bleached by the sun.

He said to me, "Son of man, can these bones live?"

I said, "Master God, only you know that."......

......God, the Master, told the dry bones, "Watch this: I'm bringing the breath of life to you and you'll come to life........You'll come alive and you'll realize that I am God!"

I prophesied just as I'd been commanded. As I prophesied, there was a sound and, oh, rustling! The bones moved and came together, bone to bone...

...Listen to what they're saying: 'Our bones are dried up, our hope is gone, there's nothing left of us.'.....

......"Therefore, prophesy. Tell them, 'God, the Master, says: I'll dig up your

graves and bring you out alive—O my people! ....I've said it and I'll do it.

God's Decree.'"

-Ezekiel 37:1-14 (MSG)

Sometimes you go through life and come to a place where you suddenly realize that there's an empty space inside of you; a broken place that has been there for so long that you've somehow managed to cover it up. You've done such a good job of ignoring it that you've almost fooled yourself into thinking it's not there. You're convinced it's better that way because if you uncover it......the pain. But deep inside you know it's there.

Maybe it was the loss of a loved one; or an abandoned dream from our youth. Possibly someone hurt you so bad it carved this pit out that exists to this day. Whatever it is, it is your valley of dry bones. It's that place where your hope of ever being healed has been stolen. That valley of brokenness that appears irreparable. But one day, at the appointed time, at the chosen place, there's a sound, and then, a rustling.....

One night God blessed me by allowing me to watch this Scripture take place right before my very eyes! Our Church had lost power and so we moved our service outside. As worship progressed something different started to happen. Young people started going up to the altar. One by one they started making their way forward, raising their hands, praying, and being prayed for. Suddenly the wave started. They started breaking. The tears started flowing and it was right then that I knew that they were being restored. They were opening up that hidden valley of dry, broken bones and they were exchanging them for breathes of life. The bones were living and God was keeping His Word. Hurts were being healed! And you know how I knew this was truly

happening. My loved ones were among those being healed.
And with that, I was being healed too....

I am tempted to say that you needed to be there to understand. But the reality of it is that it wasn't about the location. It was about the presence...the Presence of God. And you know what is so amazing? It's this Presence that is there for all of us; this internal healing power that can reach into the deepest, darkest places of our souls and bring light. And guess what? Where there's light the darkness disappears. All I can say is "taste of the Lord and see that He is good." Don't live another day in the Valley of Dry Bones.

Lord,
This is why you came, to heal the brokenhearted, to set the captive free, to declare your day of hope and restoration. Help us to see that Lord. Help us not to hide our brokenness and to allow your healing.
Break us to mend us. Then we will know that you are God.
Amen.

To God be the Glory

God's Message:

"Don't let the wise brag of their wisdom.

Don't let heroes brag of their exploits.

Don't let the rich brag of their riches.

If you brag, brag of this and this only:

That you understand and know me.

I'm God, and I act in loyal love.

I do what's right and set things right and fair,

and delight in those who do the same things.

These are my trademarks."

God's Decree.

-Jeremiah 9:24 (MSG)

Any football fanatics out there? Well, I don't know if I'm a fanatic but I do like the sport. I will say this, when it comes to football, I've proven that I'm faithful. Every year I patiently await the start of a new season and then I faithfully pull out all my garb and proudly proclaim that this is it, this is the year the Raiders are going to win the Super bowl!!! And no matter what the outcome of the season is, I never lose sight of my vision, this will be the year my beloved Raiders GO ALL THE WAY!!!! JUST WIN BABY!!! So a prophetic word…..watch out for the Silver and Black(okay, maybe I better watch it before I'm labeled a false prophet but….you get my point ☺).

Even when the Raiders don't make the post season, which has been unfortunately most of my days, I still enjoy watching the teams compete for an opportunity to be called the best of the best, an opportunity, an instant, where all the hard work pays off. Where what you do is culminated into a moment and in that moment no one can argue that you are at the top of your game. You are the world champions and no one is above you. Or is there someone…..

This year I enjoyed the super bowl like I typically do, even if it's just for the hoopla and the food that come with the day. Maybe it's just a reason for a celebration and I simply love celebrations. All my kids and their significant others gather and it's a party. The excitement in the air, the aura that surrounds it, is awesome. Whoever wins or loses it's a good time. For me anyway, my wife may not share this enthusiasm. But this year I enjoyed something more than the game, I enjoyed the interviews afterwards, one in particular. I'm not sure if you caught it but after having scored two touchdowns and being a major contributor to Green Bay's success, Greg Jennings stood before millions of fans worldwide and proclaimed, "To God be the glory!" Wow! To God be the glory. I loved it. Here was a man who amidst the splendor of the moment realized that there _was_ someone above him, God. And that his victory, his talent, his blessings were a gift from God. And he knew that it wasn't all about him, it was all about Him. What a breath of fresh air. Amidst a sea of ego and self righteousness one man stood out and said, "To God be the glory." What more can I say. Lord, never let me forget that if there is any reason to boast, it is in you. Can I say it one more time, To God be the Glory!

Be blessed in all He has for you!!

E Komo Mai
(Welcome Into His House)

"And let us not neglect our meeting together, as some people do, but

encourage one another, especially now that the day of his return is

drawing near."

Hebrews 10:25 (NLT)

Where do I begin? This morning I find myself in paradise. Well, okay not really paradise as Jesus would call it (and I know His version is much, much better), but it is still a place of great beauty. It is six in the morning and my eyes opened to a tropical, palm tree lined beach with an amazing view of spectacular clear blue water. As I glance at the rippling waves I am reminded of how truly magnificent creation is. My vision goes to the horizon as the first glimpses of sunlight stream through and my breath is almost taken away. This place called Hawaii is truly magnificent.

There is so much to do, so much to see, where to start. Pearl Harbor is a must. Hananuma Bay and snorkeling can't be left out. Diamond Head Crater, Polynesian Culture Center, Waikiki Beach, the list goes on and on. But then I am reminded, I am reminded of how truly blessed I am to be here and one place gets added to the list. My Father's House.

Church. I don't know if I even like that word. That may sound funny but it just doesn't seem to carry the right meaning any more. The word reminds me of a place my mother would drag me along to. In mind I associate it with obligation. Somehow it seems almost derogatory in some way, like it's

132

something I have to do but not enjoy, Church. Then the thought comes, its not the word but the interpretation that is being applied that is the issue. Church means so much more than obligation, responsibility, and requirement. It means love. It is a place of gathering to celebrate. It is where family new and old see each other again. It is filled with wonderful singing, praise, and gratitude. It has peace and it has hope. Not because of its four walls or location but because of whose house it is. It's my Father's House and He says, "E Komo Mai, Welcome, Come In."

So I didn't just fit Church into my vacation. I visited my Heavenly Father's House and met with new family and was blessed!!! The funny thing, my "Dad" has houses everywhere, and you can tell when their His, it's the same thing, "Welcome, Come in..."

Today I leave you with the hopes that we will never forget to visit this wonderful home and a prayer my brothers taught me in Hawaii:

Ho'onani ka Makua mau
(Praise God from whom all blessings flow)

Ke Keiki me ka 'Uhane no
(Praise Him all creatures here below)

Ke Akua mau ho'omaikai pu
(Praise Him above ye heavenly host)

Ko keia ao, ko kela ao
(Praise Father, Son, and Holy Ghost)

Amene

May you be as blessed, even more blessed, than I.

⁓ *The Gentle Whisper* ⁓

"Go out and stand before me on the mountain," the LORD told him. And as

Elijah stood there, the LORD passed by, and a mighty windstorm hit the

mountain. It was such a terrible blast that the rocks were torn loose, but the

LORD was not in the wind. After the wind there was an earthquake, but the

LORD was not in the earthquake. And after the earthquake there was a fire,

but the LORD was not in the fire. And after the fire there was the sound of a

gentle whisper*. When Elijah heard it, he wrapped his face in his cloak and*

went out and stood at the entrance of the cave.

And a voice (The Lord) said, "What are you doing here, Elijah?"

-1 Kings 19:11-13 (NLT)

Arrive in San Francisco and there is one thing for sure, this city is busy! As any of you who have ever driven here know, just getting into the City can be a challenge. The traffic jams, the lane changes, the 7 mile stretch which can take 45 minutes to maneuver....

Then once you arrive it doesn't change. I found myself in the Financial District in the midst of skyscrapers and people. I checked into my room and immediately I went to the window to check out the view.

As I looked down onto New Montgomery Street the busyness was even more evident. The people were covering every inch of the sidewalk and if it were not for the stop lights there wouldn't be a second to cross the road. The horns were honking, the sirens were blaring, the City was definitely bustling.

But on one particular morning I woke up before sunrise and I looked out the window again. A transformation had taken place. It was quiet. As I looked up and down the street I saw only one or two people and an occasional car. I realized that even this symbol of hustle and bustle had its still moments. But I also knew that it was simply a momentary phase that would quickly pass. And as I started to settle in to write this, the cars starting passing by sooner and sooner, a siren sounded, and the people started coming out. And even these few people who were now visible were hurrying. Hurrying off as if to beat the coming wave, knowing that this was there chance to "beat the traffic...."

That's when the Lord gave me this thought; do these busy people in this busy city ever stop to listen to the gentle whisper that can bring them so much peace in the midst of what can seem like chaos, in the midst of their busy, busy lives? But as God often does, He then directed the question back to me; do I stop often enough in my busy, busy life to listen to the gentle whisper?

You know, I can sit here and look out this window and say to myself that I surely wouldn't want to live in the midst of this fast pace world....that I'm glad that I live in the slower pace Central Valley of California and the even slower pace of my small city. But the reality of it is that my life is probably not that different as those that I see rushing around below me. There are too many times when I know that the same spirit that drives these people to be in such a rush also drives me and that more often than I care to admit, I also don't stop to listen to the gentle whisper....

There have been times where I've found myself in the same place as Elijah, running through life and running from problems. And during these times, if I do look for God, I am expecting to hear from him in the big things, the strong winds, the earthquakes, the fires. I'm still rushing around even in my quest to hear from Him. And He's patiently waiting for me to settle down so I can stop and listen to His still, small voice, His gentle whisper......shhhhhh........stop.......listen..........there it is........ At first it's hard to make out. But then it becomes clearer and clearer until suddenly: The Voice of God. And just as suddenly: Peace!!!

This morning I am thankful because God once again slowed me down and allowed me to hear his voice, even in the midst of one of busiest cities in the world. And I am even more thankful because I know He can speak to you in the same way too. Just slow down, find a quiet place, stop, spend time, and listen. He still speaks today and He wants to speak into your life.

Today be blessed and listen to the gentle whisper!

⚜ *The Mountaintop* ⚜

"GOD said to Moses, "Climb higher up the mountain and wait there for me; I'll give you tablets of stone, the teachings and commandments that I've written to instruct them." So Moses got up, accompanied by Joshua his aide. And Moses climbed up the mountain of God.

-Exodus 24:12-13 (MSG)

Every year my son and I go on our own adventure during his summer break. We've gone to many different places, caves and caverns, gold-mining towns, ocean beaches, but this year he had chosen the spot. This year he wanted to go to the Mountaintop. The mountaintop I speak of is a local peak called Mt. Diablo.

It all started one day when my wife, my son and I were coming back from the bay area and decided we wanted to stop somewhere. The closest state park was Mt. Diablo and despite its name, off we went. As we were approaching the Mountain, it really didn't appear very treacherous and it definitely didn't seem to live up to its name. But as we started on this little journey, the road to the top started to get longer and longer, and higher and higher. Now you have to know that my wife has this great fear of heights and the fact that she had agreed to go on this venture was surprising to say the least. And if the truth must be told, I'm not too fond of driving cliff-hanging roads myself. But of course, with my son egging us on, we pressed ahead. We pressed

137

ahead until we got to this spot where a sign stated, "Prepare to Stop." As we crept around the bend, we saw why......the edge of the road had broken off and collapsed down the mountainside. There was only enough road left for one car to squeeze through this two lane road!!

We really couldn't do anything but press ahead since turning around was impossible, so press ahead we did. On we went until the next sign said we still had 7 miles to reach the top. My nerves had had it, so, being the man that I am, I stepped up and told my son, "I'm sorry but your mom is really scared, we're gonna have to turn around." He didn't buy it and proceeded to tell me it was me who was chickening out, but of course I insisted I was looking out for his beloved mother and back down the mountain we went, never reaching our goal of making it to the mountaintop.

Well, all of that brings us back to beginning of my story. Weeks later when I asked my son where he would want to go for our day together, he quickly said, "I want to go to the top of Mt. Diablo" with a smile. I swallowed slowly and asked him if he was sure since there were so many wonderful places we could go besides this barren mountain but he just smiled back and said, "Man up Dad!"

Being the brave father that I am, we packed up and off we went. As we approached the mountain I was determined not to let my son see even a smidgen of my anxiety but he knows me all to well and every once in a while he looked at me with a wry smile on his face, kind of giggling. Finally we hit the same 7 mile sign. It was really here that the adventure started. This was new land, unchartered territory, the place where we (or should I say I) had faltered and retreated. This time I was determined to go where no man had gone before ☺. After a quick conversation between myself and God, we proceeded. We proceeded and before I knew it, we conquered!! We made it to the mountaintop and it was magnificent!!!

I turned to my son with a great big grin and I said, "We did it!!" He smiled back and said, "Yes you did Dad, yes you did…" From here the time was priceless. As we walked to the overview, we looked out and took in the beauty of the Livermore Valley. We went over to the other side and spotted the Antioch Bridge which we had crossed to get here. The Delta meandered through the land and the hills and valleys were phenomenal. From this viewpoint we saw the land we had travelled so many times from a very different perspective. We saw it from God's perspective. As we started down a trail, we saw a wooden terrace which had been built to hang over the mountainside and give you a grand view of the surrounding area. As we sat on the bench, we were both quiet and suddenly the realization of the moment hit. Here we were, having pushed the boundaries, having accomplished something together, with no one else around but me, my son, and God. I looked at my son and we both bowed our heads and prayed together giving thanks for this moment together. Words can't describe this moment.

By now I'm hoping you can see the life lesson in this story. Had we (or should I say I) never pushed my boundaries and reached for more, we never would have experienced the grandeur before us and that priceless moment. It made me realize how much there is to life right in our immediate surrounding. I had seen this mountain all my life, lived within an hours drive of it, and had never stopped to experience it. Now add to this the value of time spent bonding with my boy and the experience becomes immeasurable. Finally, the pinnacle of the moment, realizing we had God to thank for it!

Now to you a simple drive up to the top of Mt. Diablo may not be a big thing. But what are the areas that God is pushing you to expand your boundaries? What are the mountaintops that He has placed before you? God showed me something, you can't have a mountaintop experience without climbing the mountain first. Sounds simple but how many times had I stood at the base of things only wishing I could reach the top. Thinking it was out of my reach when all along it was attainable. He also showed me the value of quality time spent with the ones we love. This was a moment my son will never forget. Someday he may take his own son on this journey and tell him of the day we went together. Once again, priceless!!!

On this day I reached my mountaintop and shared the moment with my son.

On any day you can reach yours.

Today, be blessed....

ᶜᵛᵛ **Silence of the Lord** ᶜᵛᵛ

"For here's what God told me: "I'm not going to say anything, but simply look on from where I live, Quiet as warmth that comes from the sun, silent as dew during harvest." And then, just before harvest, after the blossom has turned into a maturing grape, He'll step in and prune back the new shoots"
-Isaiah 18:3-5

There was a time where I suddenly found myself empty, waiting for God to "speak". Not only to put something into my heart to write about but also to speak into others areas of my life but... nothing. Nothing but silence.

It was strange because I had just come off of a phenomenal week where He had spoken volumes to me and took me to new levels of my walk with Him. At first I didn't think too much of it but then after a couple of days I started to long for His personal Word. I did all of the same things I had done the week before but I wasn't breaking through. I started reading and saw that as God He had the right to be silent and it wasn't my place to question Him (as Job found out) but still it wasn't about questioning Him. It was about being with Him. I continued on in faith knowing He hadn't left me but still longing for that intimacy. Last night my wife came home from a prayer meeting and, being my wife, she knew something was wrong and she began to pray for me. It was amazing! She truly brought the presence of God into our home and I loved her for it because God broke some things in my life....but still it wasn't my intimacy. And then it happened.

141

I woke up one morning and jumped up to find my son. All week he had been reminding me that today was his birthday and all week I had been silent on the subject. In my heart I was as excited as he was but I wanted to save that excitement for this blessed morning. And it was a blessing!! I jumped on him and we hugged and I knew that in that instant he knew how much he meant to me. It was a great morning!

I settled in and suddenly God spoke!! I read the Scripture above from Isaiah, I contemplated, and I heard "Happy Birthday". In my spirit God reminded me of that moment 15 years ago today when I had surrendered all to Him and how He had taken a broken life and given me back joy, peace, and contentment. And today He "hugged" me and in that instant I knew how much I meant to Him!

Now I know the intimacy of silence. I know that where there is love, silence makes the heart grow fonder. I know that in that silence God is trusting me to know He is still there. I also see that if the heart is right, silence produces longing and longing is a sign of true love. And best of all, I know that the silence is never forever. And when it's broken, what joy!!!!

Today I am a blessed man because God has entrusted me with this wonderful revelation!! I pray you allow Him to entrust you with it too...

Lord
Thank you for always being with us even when we don't hear or sense you. Help us during those times, no matter how long they may be, to never lose sight of you. Thank you for your Word which assures us that at the right moment you will always move and be heard. Today we trust in this.
Amen.

"When you cannot hear God, you will find that He has trusted you in the most intimate way possible—with

absolute silence, not a silence of despair, but one of pleasure, because He saw that you could withstand an even bigger revelation."
-Oswald Chambers

Rain, Rain Go Away

" For everything there is a season,

a time for every activity under heaven.

A time to be born and a time to die.

A time to plant and a time to harvest.

A time to kill and a time to heal.

A time to tear down and a time to build up.

A time to cry and a time to laugh.

A time to grieve and a time to dance."

-Ecclesiastes 3:1-4 (NLT)

This year I began to get really excited about the weather early on in mid February. As I drive to work, I pay close attention to my surroundings and one day I saw a beautiful sight. As I came around a curve, suddenly there sat before me a field of white. White blossoms on beautiful white almond trees. It was magnificent. I started looking closer and this phenomena was everywhere. There were trees with pinkish hues and bushes with slightly red buds. The birds were singing just a little bit happier this morning and the sun was shining just a little bit warmer. The grass was growing and the flowers were blooming and I thought to myself, "I love spring!!!"

Then I remembered it was mid February. When I mentioned my joy of the early season to someone, they agreed it was beautiful but what about the rain? I thought back and couldn't actually remember a true storm this year. I couldn't remember, and in fact didn't even realize, we had just gone through winter. It seemed as if winter skipped us and we went from fall to spring. This started giving me concerns. What was happening with the irregularity of our seasons? What if we didn't get rain? What good would the beauty of white blossoms be if the tree didn't produce the fruit it was supposed to because it lacked the vitality of the rain? I remembered and I knew, there's a season for everything and even though I love the spring, we need the winter too.

Isn't this like our lives? I know I love it when everything is shining in my life. When everything around me is blossoming and the birds are singing and the sun is shining. Wouldn't it be great if from the moment of birth life just went perfect for all of us and the problems or dark times of "winter" were never known? Would it? The more I reflect, the more I think no. I need a little rain. It has its purpose and it produces its fruit. During "winter" seasons in my life I grow stronger. It develops endurance and hope. It brings cleansing and much needed water to my soul. It reminds me that this life is a whole book not just chapters of good times. There are dry seasons, wet seasons, devastating seasons, and seasons of joy. But all in all, the seasons fold in to one experience and that experience is life!!

Today, the area I live in is coming out of a week long storm. The irregular, early warm days are gone and it has been wet, cold and windy......and I'm glad. We needed it. I needed it. Now I can sit back and look forward to the joy of the spring days again but give thanks for the needed winter days as well. After all, what would we have to look forward to if all we knew was spring?

Thank you Lord for the blessings of every "time" in our lives!
In Jesus name we pray,
Amen.

 *Pioneers*

"Unless the LORD had been my help,

My soul would soon have settled in silence."

-Psalm 94:17 (NKJV)

Recently I got to spend a wonderful day exploring the Gold Rush towns in the foothills east of us. On this adventure, we came across a "ghost town" called Campo Seco. Within this town was an old cemetery from the 1800s so we stopped to take a look. As we were walking, I came to a headstone for a man named Hugh Huston from the Broch Parish of Donegal, Ireland. He had left this Earth in 1864. It made me stop and think of what this place must have been like then and how far this man had ventured during a time when jets didn't get you there in a matter of hours. This man was a pioneer. He had pushed himself further and not given up on a dream even when I'm sure he had many opportunities to settle. I wondered if because of his efforts his descendants, and even us, were now reaping the rewards of his sacrifice. Then last night's message at service brought Mr. Huston back to my mind.

Lately, I have been feeling pioneerish (if there's such a word) myself. I am blessed to be a part of a start-up school and am helping to lay the foundation and structure for those to come. I believe God is with me and those around me and is going to bless all of our efforts. However, God reminded me last night that He is not a settler, nor should I be. While I am pushing forward with this vision at work, I was made aware that I must always be pushing forward with all the other areas of my life. Striving to make my marriage better, to build my relationships with my family and my Lord, to push forward in the things I do for God and to never "settle" in any area of my life. We are meant always to be pioneers. Wow! What a perspective. What an outlook on life. Can you imagine if we truly did this? How blessed our lives would be! Happier families, richer relationships, flourishing homes, communities, jobsites and churches!!

At the end of the day, I know I can't do this alone. That's why I love this Scripture: "Unless the LORD had been my help,
My soul would soon have settled in silence.".

As we were leaving, we came upon another tombstone and it read,

"Born into Earth...1834,
Born into Heaven..1887"

This person never settled.
Lord, help us never to settle in our lives!!

Be blessed today!!!!

 *Friends*

"Be good friends who love deeply...."

-Romans 12:10a (MSG)

No I'm not talking about the TV sitcom. And actually I don't feel like I have any deep revelations. Just a special appreciation for the relationships God has blessed each and every one of us with: friendships.

These relationships gather throughout our lives and come in many variations. There are those very special childhood friendships. It's funny because as I write this my mind takes me back to elementary school and a kid who lived across the street from me. We were nothing alike: he loved sports, I loved books; he was outgoing and loud; I was quiet and shy (believe that ☺); he ate casseroles (he was white), I ate tacos (Mexican). We would argue about everything but yet he was my best friend. And during that time he made a lasting impression in my mind. So lasting that even though I haven't seen him in 35 years, when I was asked to list my first friend as a security question for a password, it was his name that I typed in.

Then there are those teenage/young adult friends we gather in life. I'm not talking about the many "acquaintances" we come to know, but those true friends who even though you may not see them often, sometimes not for years, when you do see them it's as if you were never apart and your friendship hasn't diminished one bit. You know the ones I'm talking about. The ones who have those wild stories about you, so wild that when you talk you're half tempted to shoo the wife or kids away because you don't know what will come out of their mouths. But at the same time it's those wonderful memories of times past that drives this special bond between you. Recently, I got to sit a table with three of these special friends I'm speaking of and I was truly blessed and thankful. We had all gone our separate ways and led very different lives but at that moment we were all transported back in time to the days of our youth and even if it was only for a few minutes, it felt good. Unfortunately too often these gatherings happen at events like funerals and we're also reminded of the lost friends who are no longer with us and they deserve a moment of silence.......

Then there are the friends we gather at work who become special to us since we spend so many hours of the day with them. For me there have been those special work relationships which have crossed that line and become special personal friends and you know who you are. I am thankful for each of you.

And of course you can't forget the people who by definition are family but in spirit are true friends. We know that blood alone does not make a friendship but when the two are combined it is a unique and wonderful blend. In this case I am especially talking about my wife who has become the best friend a man could ever wish for. This is a treasure from Heaven.

150

There are friends we gather from church, from the neighborhood, from the local store, but where ever they come from, they are blessings from God. Stop today and tell one of those friends how much you appreciate them. Tell them how much of an impact they've made on your life. And finally thank God that He sent them into your life. Because of this crossing of paths, you will never be the same. Today, if you are reading this, I am giving thanks for you. You are my encouragement and my hope and I know that when God wakes me up at 5 am to write these thoughts, they are not in vain. Together we will share and treasure this life and together we will be thankful for each other.

Today,
Be Blessed!

Ps. I've got to put in a plug for Facebook. I know some may think it's a waste of time, and I've got to admit it can be, but it has blessed me with the renewing of old friendships so…..
Just my thought, see you there! ☺

❧ **Free At Last** ❧

"Therefore if the Son makes you free, you shall be free indeed."

-John 8:36 (KJV)

What a wonderful thing it is be free. To have freedom. To be able to choose the course of our lives and have opportunity to see that course completed. But freedom never comes without a price.

Abraham Lincoln was a man who knew that price. Many don't know that before he made it to the White House he had failed at virtually every endeavor. When he arrived, he found a nation divided. When he sought God and answered the call to stop slavery, he saw a nation devastated.
When he experienced victory, he felt the pain of its cost and said,

"With malice toward none, with charity for all, with firmness in the right as God gives us to see the right, let us strive on to finish the work we are in, to bind up the nation's wounds, to care for him who shall have borne the battle and for his widow and his orphan, to do all which may achieve and cherish a just and lasting peace among ourselves and with all nations."
(Abraham Lincoln Second Inaugural Address)

Within a month after these words, he would lose his life.

Martin Luther King went to Montgomery, Alabama with the thought of pastoring a quiet church and finishing his studies. He didn't know that shortly after his arrival, Rosa Parks would sit on a bus and his destiny would be changed. He also took the call of God and saw a nation divided. But he pressed in and against bitter opposition and hatred stood firm in his non-violent approach against an injustice to his people. Even after arrest and bombing. He stood and believed so much in his purpose that he said,

"Well, I don't know what will happen now. We've got some difficult days ahead. But it doesn't matter with me now. Because I've been to the mountaintop. And I don't mind. Like anybody, I would like to live a long life. Longevity has its place. But I'm not concerned about that now. I just want to do God's will. And He's allowed me to go up to the mountain. And I've looked over. And I've seen the Promised Land. I may not get there with you. But I want you to know tonight, that we, as a people, will get to the promised land. And I'm happy, tonight. I'm not worried about anything. I'm not fearing any man. Mine eyes have seen the glory of the coming of the Lord."
(I've Been to the Mountaintop by Martin Luther King, Jr.)

The next day he was murdered.

And the ultimate freedom fighter: Jesus. He stood against the rulers of His day and opposed the status quo. He loved the despised and set in motion a new way of life which, over 2,000 years later, is still changing hearts. He came to a place, in a garden when he was about to accept His calling, in the midst of sweating blood said,

"Abba, Father, everything is possible for you. Please take this cup of suffering

away from me. Yet I want your will to be done, not mine."

-Mark 14:36 (NLT)

He arose, took up His cross, and laid down His life for our freedom.
Freedom from ourselves. Freedom from our sins. Freedom from the burdens of this life. True freedom of the heart! And in the end said,

"It is finished!"

And it is. The road has been paved. The way made clear. The price paid. But the choice still remains. What will you do with your life?
Will you lay down your life and give it to Him? Will you walk in this freedom? Will you join me in repeating those immortal words,

"Free at last! Free at last! Thank God Almighty, we are free at last!"
(I Have a Dream by Martin Luther King, Jr.)

Lord,
You paid the ultimate price and in love endured the cross. And you ask that we simply have faith in your sacrifice. Thank you for this precious gift. Let us all see its value and lay down our lives as well. What you give us in return will far surpass what we lay down for you.

Thank you!

Conclusion

If you've made it this far through my endeavor you've "walked" through a year of my life week by week. There were days that were full of hope and joy; then there were days of difficulty and sorrow. But all in all, there were days, days that I've been blessed to experience and days that I've been blessed to share. As this literary adventure comes to an end, life continues. However, there is one thing that I had to convey before you left. Take a glance back at the cover. Put yourself on that beautiful trail and notice how green and plush everything is around you. In the horizon is a tree full of knowledge and experience. You keep walking towards it but you never quite arrive. That's because knowledge is a life long pursuit. You take a look above and all you can see is the great expanse we call the sky. It seems to change from golden to blue hues and you're reminded of how vast life is and how it changes "color" from time to time, light to dark. You suddenly realize that you can't quite see where this trail leads but there is one clear direction it follows. It continuously winds back and forth towards the Son. Though sometimes it get's dark and sometimes it's cloudy, somehow you always come back to this beautiful green field with the amazing tree before you and the Son always rising. It is this vision that keeps you going. It is this hope that keeps life worth living. It is this mindset that allows you to see what I see. The Son....

While I hope that you found words of encouragement on this adventure, I hope even more that you found the one thing that will change your life forever, the Son,

Jesus. It is Jesus who is the light of the world. It is Jesus who guides our path. It is Jesus who came to give us the ultimate knowledge of God. And it is Jesus who will keep our pastures green. Never forget Jesus. He will never forget you…..

Blessings!!!

Notes

Notes

Notes